STo

1-27-77

White Gold

ALSO BY DEREK WILSON

A Tudor Tapestry

WHITE GOLD

The Story of African Ivory

Derek Wilson

AND

Peter Ayerst

TAPLINGER PUBLISHING COMPANY

NEW YORK

First published in the United States in 1976 by
TAPLINGER PUBLISHING CO., INC.
New York, New York

Library of Congress Catalog Card Number: 76-363
ISBN 0-8008-8251-2

Contents

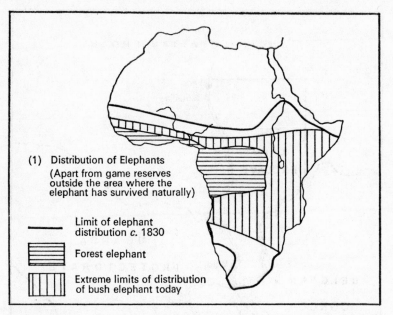

(1) Distribution of Elephants
(Apart from game reserves outside the area where the elephant has survived naturally)

——— Limit of elephant distribution c. 1830

Forest elephant

Extreme limits of distribution of bush elephant today

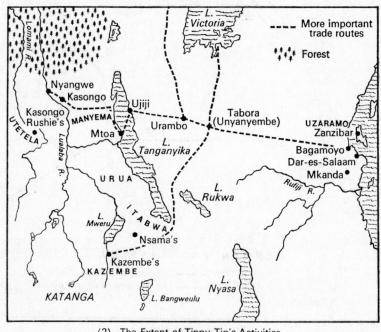

- - - More important trade routes

Forest

(2) The Extent of Tippu Tip's Activities

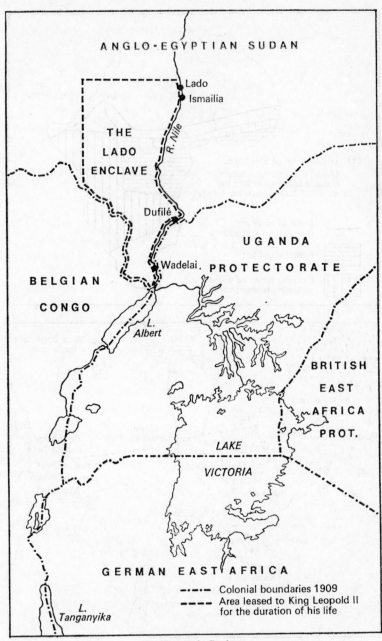

ANGLO-EGYPTIAN SUDAN

Lado
Ismailia

THE
LADO
ENCLAVE

R. Nile

Dufilé

UGANDA

Wadelai.

PROTECTORATE

BELGIAN

CONGO

L.
Albert

BRITISH

EAST

AFRICA

PROT.

LAKE

VICTORIA

GERMAN EAST AFRICA

—·—·— Colonial boundaries 1909
— — — Area leased to King Leopold II
for the duration of his life

L.
Tanganyika

(3) The Lado Enclave

1

'Nature's great master-piece, an Elephant.
The onely harmless great thing; the giant of beasts.'

—John Donne, THE PROGRESS OF THE SOUL (1612)

Elephant and Man

There can be few experiences more primeval than standing in the African bush close to a herd of elephants. Even at a 'safe' distance the animals are so immense, so powerful, that a man seems, somehow, puny. At dusk this rare experience becomes even more impressive; as the evening sun briefly throws the thorn trees into vivid yellow relief, you become suddenly aware of the noise.

A hundred elephant have come down to a waterhole, travelling correctly in line astern along the track, each baby lightly gripping its mother's tail with its trunk. Then they break ranks at the water, some drinking, others wading or wallowing, a few bulls keeping guard with trunks swinging and ears softly flapping to and fro. The brief tropical twilight fades; the vast forms merge with their background and just as gradually the noises seem to grow louder; the soft swishing of crumpled skin on skin as the beasts jostle each other; the hissing of water squirted from elephant trunks; the ear-splitting shriek of a cow trying to locate her errant calf; and beneath all the steady bass beat of a hundred gigantic rumbling bellies. You can easily imagine yourself, then, a Stone Age savage on the fringe of some ancient jungle, anxiously keeping downwind of these terrifying beasts.

The interaction of man and elephant has been a long one; and not only in Africa and Asia. Until as recently (geologically speaking) as 7,000 years ago, vast herds of elephant roamed freely in Europe and America as well. By then our ancestors were already hunting the mighty beasts. To Stone Age man an elephant was the largest single source of meat available. He represented many days' nourishment even for the largest hunter-gatherer community. Just when man began hunting elephant is impossible to say. The necessary skills were obviously developed at different times in different regions and some peoples never mastered the techniques at all.

There were elephant-like animals in the world long before anything resembling man was around to watch them. The earliest known member of the elephant order was a small pig-like animal called Moeritherium which lived nearly fifty million years ago. Moeritherium had a long snout, though not a trunk and carried four tusks, two in the upper jaw and two in the lower. The fossilised remains of these tusks suggest that they were used for digging. If nature abhors a vacuum she also eschews the spectacular—at least in terms of evolution. From this early start nature carried out many experiments on the elephant theme and some were very spectacular indeed.

A line of animals known as the Deinotherium had tusks in the lower jaw. Anacus had perfectly straight downward pointing tusks which must have been very unwieldly. A leading authority on mammal evolution has claimed that a related animal lived on in South America until as late as A.D. 200. Another line called Serridentinus had four tusks, two in each jaw; it died out over a million years ago. All of these experiments were doomed to eventual failure though some of them survived for some twenty million years. Less than ten million years ago, however, a line of elephants appeared with one pair of curving tusks in the upper jaw and a very effective design of tooth which let them feed more efficiently than any others. It is from this line that all the modern types have been produced. These magnificent animals established themselves on the plains and in the forests of the world far back in the prehistoric past and lived more or less unmolested by predators for millions of years.

Then, some three million years or more ago a new mammal appeared; one which was cleverer and more adaptable. Beside the swamps and rivers of Africa he appeared—a hairy, long armed creature, walking upright but with a forward stoop. With the emergence of man the long period of peaceful domination enjoyed by the elephant herds came to an end. Though not large, and living only in small groups, man became a menace to his neighbours because he could wield bones, clubs and lumps of stone as weapons. His awkward fingers were already in their fumbling fashion creating other tools—handaxes and scrapers—from obsidian and other easily flaked rock.

Man in this primitive early state at the dawn of the Stone Age was no threat to the elephant. He lived on plants, fish, reptiles, eggs and birds. Rarely did he have any cause to pit his stamina and cunning against the speed and strength of larger animals. Then, in time, man changed his ways. He discovered the bolus, a device of small stones and strips of skin which, if skilfully thrown, could bring down even the most fleet-footed gazelle or buck. He discovered the pit trap which, with luck, would do his catching for him while he sat at home in his rock shelter. Perhaps most momentous of all, he learned the advantages of hunting in packs with others of his kind.

This was the beginning of human society. When man lived in community with other men beyond his immediate family circle he increased his potential as a hunter. He also increased his demand for meat. More mouths to feed meant that, whenever possible, larger animals had to be caught—wildebeest, giraffe and zebra, and sometimes, in some places, elephant.

In the absence of evidence to the contrary, we may perhaps imagine how the long conflict between man and elephant began. We see a group of hunters going out to inspect their traps. They approach one of the pits from which a great noise is issuing. There is a frenzied elephant, its grey flanks streaked with earth and pulling more down on top of it in its efforts to clamber out of the deep narrow hole. Cautiously the men encircle the frantic beast, staring for a long time in fascinated silence. Then one, braver than the rest, hurls his bone-tipped spear. It pierces the thick skin to no great depth but the massive brute lifts its trunk in a shrill cry of anger and pain. The hunters rush into the cover of the bush, only to return slowly, cautiously. They realise now that the elephant cannot hurt them. Emboldened by this knowledge they seize spears, rocks and boulders to hurl down on to the trapped animal. Blood flecks the heaving flanks, one eye becomes a red pulpy mess and frenzy seizes the hunters. They rush back and forth with fresh missiles, their exultant shouts mingling with the roars and squeals of the long-dying elephant. Hours later the conflict comes to an end and the hunters fling themselves on the carcase, gouging out the flesh with their clumsy axes. The work goes quickly as the hunters gather as much meat as they can, for other scavengers will be on the kill as soon as the men leave. For several days after the battle the men and their families gorge themselves on elephant meat. There is rest from hunting and time to act over again in dance and mime the great victory of man over the mightiest of beasts.

It is easy to see why the elephant has always fascinated man the hunter. The size and the ferocity of a cornered elephant were a challenge to the bravery and skill of the pursuer. It is therefore no surprise to find elephants featured in some of the earliest known examples of African rock art. Stories, songs and dances passed down from distant antiquity still tell of this giant of the bush and man's encounter with him. Over the centuries and the millennia African man has perfected his hunting techniques, but he still regards the elephant with respect and awe. There are still hunting communities whose paintings and dances have a magical significance and, in some mystical way, give man superiority over his prey.

There is also the practical attraction of the elephant for the hunter, for he is still the largest meat supply on four legs. H. Darley, a British sportsman who went to East Africa during the golden age of the white hunter (1890–1914) recounts how, while passing through Karamoja (in present N.E. Uganda), his path was blocked by the Toposan. When Darley explained that he had only come to hunt elephant the local leaders were sceptical. 'There is a herd of elephant just beyond those hills,' they said, 'show us.' So Darley made for the browsing herd and after a while succeeded in killing two young bulls. Immediately the entire local population rushed forward and fell greedily upon the slain animals. Darley continues:

'Next morning I sent off some of my men to see if the natives had finished with the elephants. All they found were the bare skulls with the tusks sticking out of them. Every other bit of skin, meat and bone had been carried off for food and even the perforated bone in the front part of the skulls had been cut out. I believe it makes a very good soup.'

The excitement caused by the killing of an elephant or the finding of a dead one must have been even more intense in earlier times. Before the Iron Age a slain elephant represented not only a major addition to the larder (man soon learned how to preserve meat by cutting it into strips and drying it in the sun) but also copious raw material for tools, weapons and clubs. The skin, the flesh, the bone, everything about the elephant had its usefulness.

In some places a local tribe would come to depend almost completely on the elephant. The remains of such an elephant-oriented society have recently been studied in some detail. Excavations of a palaeolithic settlement near Cracow in South Poland show that the people who lived there over 20,000 years ago were dependent on the northern elephant or mammoth. They built their simple houses out of mammoth bones, ate mainly mammoth meat and used its body for many artifacts; even lamps made from hollow bones have been found. The houses were particularly interesting. The foundations were made of a circle of lower jaws, large limb bones and shoulder blades firmly interlocked. Ribs and tusks were fitted in as uprights and then skins were spread across. The long curved mammoth tusks were used as main arches to hold the whole thing together. Even today there are, in Africa, several tribes whose lives are similarly bound up with elephants. These communities hunted the elephant and the mammoth for meat and skin. Proficient though they were they cannot have made much impact on the population figures of these beasts. The real conflict between man and elephant must have come when the human species settled to an agricultural life. Man then had to kill 'nature's master-piece' not only to feed his family but also to protect his crops. The elephants were driven off their former grazing grounds and moved northwards. Their numbers decreased steadily as death stalked them with two weapons—the hunter's spear and the barren rock. There is little doubt that the mammoths were an early casualty in the war between man and elephant which continues to the present day.

What would have happened if the two last elephant, the African and Asian, had disappeared along with the mammoth is one of the most fascinating historical 'ifs'. The story of man would have been very different. Without the massive working elephant of India, which can be tamed and made to carry, push and pull to order, the development of that sub-continent must have been slower. Without ivory there would have been little to lure 'get-rich-quick' Arab and European adventurers into the heart of Africa. Probably parts of that continent would still be unexplored. Certainly the colonial scramble for Africa would have taken a much different form.

The African elephant is an astonishing beast. He has inspired the respect and even the affection of all men who have come into close contact with him. Until two thousand years ago there were herds over most of Africa and even today, after many centuries of indiscriminate hunting, it has been estimated that there are at least three hundred thousand left. What is it about this magnificent beast that has made him so successful?

In the first place he is a very large and powerful animal. He is far and away the largest extant land animal and is among the largest that has every lived.* A large bull elephant may stand over 11 feet at the shoulder and weigh six tons. A giant shot in Angola in 1955 was 13 feet 2 inches at the shoulder and weighed nearly 12 tons. Not only are elephants of enormous size, they are very strong and active. They frequently walk up to 30 miles a day to and from water and are believed to be capable of a speed of about 25 miles per hour over a short distance.

A further important factor in the success of elephants is their intelligence. There is a great deal of argument about this, but then, intelligence is a very difficult thing to define and an even more difficult thing to test in a wild animal. What about the elephant's fabled long memory?

> 'Prince, a precept I leave for you,
> Coined in Eden, existing yet:
> Skirt the parlor, and shun the zoo,
> Women and elephants never forget.'

There are certainly many stories which seem to add point to

---

* The large dinosaurs are excluded here because, despite their size, they were not bulky animals and in any case spent most of their lives in water where their weight was supported.

Dorothy Parker's advice, but the presence of a long memory does not necessarily denote intelligence. The elephant has the largest brain of any land animal that has ever lived; it weighs over ten pounds. In relation to its body bulk, however, this is not very much. For instance, taken as a percentage of body weight it is about one-tenth the size of the human brain. Nevertheless in relation to many other animals this is still a respectable size and is not inconsistent with intelligence.

A useful pointer to intelligence is an animal's range of emotion. Here among animals the elephant is outstanding. It is, of course, easy to be anthropomorphic and to credit the animal with human emotions simply because of facial expressions which, in the elephant, have very different meanings. Ivan Sanderson tells of Sadie, an elephant being trained for the circus in Lancaster, Missouri, who could not understand a trick. She tried to escape and was punished, whereupon she lay down and cried, 'She lay there on her side, the tears streaming down her face and sobs racking her huge body.'

Jean Pierre Hallet, who hunted elephants in the Congo, said:

'I have more than once seen forest elephants, extremely drunk after gobbling up vast quantities of fermenting fruit, giggling with delight as they lobbed pieces of squishy fruit at each other's heads and derrieres.'

This sort of tale, and there are many of them, leaves no doubt that the elephant is capable of many moods. Other evidence comes from stories of the behaviour of elephants in the wild when faced with situations which are unusual and therefore unlikely to have been encountered previously and learned by experience. A common hunter's tale concerns the help which elephants will give to other members of the herd. W. Robert Foran, who hunted with gun and camera in Africa for nearly fifty years, described such an incident. A close friend, Frank H. Melland was hunting elephants in the Luangwa Valley of Zambia. He shot a large bull in the region of the heart but failed to kill it outright.

'Although neither Melland nor his African gunbearer heard any signal of distress from this wounded bull, one must have been made, for five of the animals halted immediately and returned to help it escape from the river bed. He watched what happened and refrained from shooting again, being too much enthralled in observing the incident.

'Two of the rescue party got their shoulders to either flank of the wounded bull; another couple of cows pressed sideways against them; and an aged cow got her massive head under the bull's stern to shove it forwards and upwards. Melland said that the affair resembled the back row of a scrum in rugby football. Somehow the five of them succeeded in heaving the bull up a precipitous crumbling 50-foot-high river bank and over the crest; then all of them disappeared beyond the bank.'

This is obviously an intelligent response on the part of a group of animals to an unprecedented situation. Such tales are not rare; almost every book of African hunter reminiscences contains similar stories.

Some scientific studies have been made by animal psychologists using zoo and circus animals. The general consensus of opinion is that the elephant is indeed a clever animal. This is all the more remarkable because herbivorous animals are almost never intelligent. As a general rule it is meat-eating animals which develop mental proficiency as a result of having to use their wits to catch their prey. Why then should the elephant be an exception? The answer is almost certainly because of the presence of a trunk.

Not only is the trunk a strong, agile organ easily capable of breaking branches off trees, it is also a very sensitive and delicate one. The tip has two finger-like extensions and with these it can perform such delicate operations as picking up individual coins from the floor. Not only is the trunk a part of the very sensitive nostril it also acts as both an arm and a hand. It has been argued by competent biologists that the mental powers of man are partly the result of the evolution of his sensitive and mobile hands, which provide him with very detailed information through his sense of touch and permit very delicate manoeuvring of objects. The same arguments hold good for the elephant and its trunk.

Apart from keen senses and intelligence, an animal needs an effective food collecting apparatus to survive. It has the best chance of success if it can collect food not generally available to other animals, as it will therefore have no competition. The elephant, with its seven-foot-long, flexible trunk, can stretch high into trees and pick off succulent leaves which few other animals can reach. It also uses its trunk for drinking. The tip is placed in water and about two gallons drawn up. The tip is then put in the mouth and the water blown out and swallowed. It is, of course, impossible for a human (or any other mammal) to blow out and swallow at the same time. In order to do it, the elephant has had to develop a special set of extra chest muscles.

Elephants have been known to survive without a trunk. Occasionally the organ may be damaged by snares and if gangrene sets in, after great pain it may be lost. Although the animal may survive it is often dependent on others of its herd. Jean Pierre Hallet describes such a beast and at the same time gives further evidence of intelligent responses to unusual situations:

'As they settled down to browse in a thicket of Mimosa I watched the trunkless elephant stand idly while the herd tore at the trees gathering twigs and leaves. None of them ate so much as a single leaf but moved instead towards their handicapped companion, bearing bundles of food, as they must have done for several years. He opened his mouth expectantly. Eager to feed him first, two of the elephants jostled each other. The rest waited their turns patiently. In all they brought the trunkless welfare case so much food that he hardly had time to chew it.'

There is no evidence of how this animal managed to drink. Presumably he was assisted by the herd in the same way. As an elephant may require up to fifty gallons a day this was no mean task.

Probably the most important reason of all for the success of the elephant, however, is its complex but well balanced social life. From the moment it is born the elephant is integrated into a closely knit society which is as important to it as the society of other people is to a human child.

Elephants normally move in small family groups of about a dozen. Each group is a separate matriarchal society, the leader being the oldest cow that is still capable of breeding. Each group will consist of her adult female offspring together with young animals of both sexes and possibly a few 'retired' animals. The adult bulls wander off on their own and occasionally become attached to other herds though they never become a permanent part of them. It is physically impossible for larger herds than this to exist for long because the surrounding country quickly becomes depleted of their fodder. Sometimes travellers have seen very large herds, over a hundred strong, but such congregations are very rare. In 1934 Rennie Bere, later to become chief game warden of Uganda, described such a herd most evocatively:

> 'Acres and acres of elephants—large elephants, small elephants, bulls, cows and calves. Some were quiet, others playful, some feeding and others waving their trunks about in the air and screaming; and the whole time the interminable thunderous rumble of their bellies—it was a sight, at any rate the first time you see it, that has to be seen to be believed.'

It used to be thought that elephants only bred in secret and that mating and birth occur in a few hidden localities. This is a very old fallacy. Pliny (A.D. 23–79) in his *Natural History* says:

> 'Elephants are sensible to feelings of modesty, they never couple but in secret.'

As they have no clear-cut breeding season in tropical Africa, mating is in fact rarely seen by the casual viewer. It has often been observed by naturalists however and is fully documented. Elephants often show great affection for each other. The bull may follow his cow round, caressing her with his trunk at regular intervals and the two of them may stand for long periods of time with their trunks intertwined, occasionally kissing with the tips. It would be difficult to imagine an animal with a more 'human' courtship.

The young elephant is born 22 months after mating, and, as one would expect after such a long gestation period, it is very large. The newly born calf is about 3 feet high at the shoulder and can weigh 17 stone. As is the case with most herbivores, the baby elephant is able to walk almost immediately after being born. This is obviously important to its survival when animals such as the lion, hyena and hunting dog inhabit the same area and are attracted by the afterbirth. The baby is further protected by the social system. Just before birth occurs, another elephant comes to help the mother-to-be, often assisting in the birth and looking after the young one until the mother is ready. Both elephants are very attentive to the baby and it is not allowed to stray from between their legs.

The baby suckles its mother for about two years, growing rapidly on the very rich milk. At one time it was virtually impossible to rear orphaned baby elephants because cow's milk was used which is not a rich enough diet for them. Elephant's milk is about one hundred times as rich in albumen (protein) as cow's milk. The first successful rearing of orphaned elephants had to wait until Major Pretorius of Johannesburg developed a feeding formula which consisted of one gallon of cow's milk plus half a pint of thick cream, the whites of 24 eggs and four pounds of overboiled rice.

Like most mammals the baby elephant has milk teeth while the jaw is growing; these include small milk tusks an inch or two long which are lost at about two years when the permanent teeth, including tusks, begin to develop.

The two dominant species in Africa, elephant and man, have a remarkably similar development, quite different from that of any other animal. The brain of both types develops very slowly which gives a long childhood. In a social animal this means a long period of family care, which is associated with intelligence. Like man, the elephant will remain with his family for about fifteen years.

Puberty occurs at about twelve or thirteen years though it may be delayed a long time in a population which is overcrowded. At puberty the young bulls will get ready to leave the herd to live more or less independently while the cows remain together except when they are on heat. Each cow may have ten or twelve children during her lifetime and as the gestation and lactation periods are so long she is nearly always either pregnant or lactating or both.

It used to be thought that elephants could live for hundreds of years, but this is another of the many old wives' tales that surround them. In the wild they cannot survive for long once the final set of teeth have worn down, since they can no longer feed. This is probably at about fifty or sixty years. The record in captivity is believed to be 67 years and it is very unlikely that a wild animal would live any longer than this, unprotected from parasites and diseases.

There are two distinct varieties of African elephant (*Loxodonta africana*) recognised by scientists; these are the immense bush elephants which inhabit the open plains and savannahs of East, Central and South Africa and the smaller forest elephants of the West and North. The two types are quite distinct in appearance and habit. The bush elephant is by far the larger animal with bigger, heavier, more curved tusks. It has huge triangular ears, each of which may be six feet wide. These ears are used mainly for cooling, acting as radiators which give out animal heat to the air. The blood leaving the ear may be as much as 15°C cooler than the blood entering and this helps to cool the body. A common sight in elephant country during the hot dusty afternoons is the animals standing quietly in the shade, the only movement being the ears wafting gently to and fro to keep the air around them moving. These same ears also make an awesome and frightening spectacle when the animal is charging since they are held out sideways to give an apparent width of over fifteen feet.

The forest elephant is not as large and has much smaller, more rounded ears. It is called *cyclotis* ('rounded ear') by scientists. As it is smaller in size it does not have the cooling problems of the bush type and living in thick forest it is more retiring in nature and does not depend upon frightening its enemies by charging at them. There are many other differences between the two types which are discernible on closer inspection. The bush elephant has four toenails on each of the front feet and three on the rear while the forest type (like the Asiatic elephant), has five at the front and four at the rear. The forest elephant tends to be more hairy. Another difference of prime importance is the tusks. The forest elephant has straighter, slimmer tusks which are much lighter in weight and the ivory is of poorer quality, being rather brittle.

In Africa the relationship between man and elephant has always been a violent one. This is strange when we consider that in India, Burma and Ceylon the elephant was, as early as

4,000 B.C., domesticated and has ever since carried man's burdens, borne him into war and has even been venerated in some societies. Is the African elephant untameable? The answer seems to be that the smaller, forest elephant can be trained but that the bush elephant is quite unbiddable or, at best, very unreliable. On some government stations in the Belgian Congo elephants were captured and trained quite adequately by mahouts imported from India who reported that their trainees were no more difficult than wild Asian ones. Local African mahouts were instructed very successfully and the elephants were still being used for forestry work some years after independence. Very few bush elephants have ever been kept in captivity or used for circus work and of those which have been 'tamed' some very nasty stories are told. Chang, an 8-year-old bull, was kept at Zurich Zoo in Switzerland. One day he was punished for making a disturbance and was not fed his usual titbits. An office girl from the zoo who had made friends with him took him some bread in the evening. She did not return. In the morning a human hand and toe were found among his bedding. Although Chang was reprieved, a few years later he battered his keeper to death and had to be put down by the authorities. Even the most famous elephant of all time, Jumbo, had to be sold off by London Zoo because he became unreliable and did a great deal of damage.

In their native land no attempt was made to tame Jumbo's ancestors; they were hunted for their meat. Various refinements were, in time, added to the simple pit trap; savagely pointed wooden stakes were embedded in the bottom and bells were rigged up to tell the hunters that the prey had been caught so that they could come to finish the elephant off before other members of the herd could come to his aid. For the simple pit trap was often too simple to baffle one of the most intelligent land mammals. Frequently the trapped elephant was extricated by his friends and relations who came and trampled the sides of the pit until a slope had been made up which the unfortunate could climb.

Many African communities were terrified of the elephant and left him severely alone but to others he represented more than a food supply—he was a challenge.

An extraordinary report written in the third century B.C.

describes how the peoples of Eritrea and Somalia killed elephants. The hunter hid in a tree until a suitable quarry passed beneath. Then,

'he seizes its tail with his hands and plants his feet against its left flank; he has hanging from his shoulders an axe, light enough so that a blow may be struck with one hand and yet very sharp, and grasping this in his right hand he hamstrings the elephant's right leg, raining blows upon it and maintaining the position of his own body with his left hand. They bring an astonishing swiftness to bear upon the task, since it is a contest between the two of them for their very lives. [Sometimes the elephant collapses] causing the death of the Ethiopian along with his own; sometimes squeezing the man against a rock or tree it crushes him with its weight until it kills him. Sometimes, however, the elephant in its extreme suffering, far from turning on its attacker, flees across the plain, until the man who has set his feet upon it, striking on the same place with his axe, has severed the tendons and paralysed the beast. And as soon as the beast has fallen they run together in companies, and cutting the flesh off the hind-quarters of the elephant while it is still alive, they hold a feast.'

This account would be scarcely credible were it not for the fact that similar stories spanning many centuries were recorded by visitors to the area. In more modern times the huntsman took to horseback and wielded a sword instead of an axe but hamstringing the prey was still his primary objective. Among the Somali the single-handed slaughter of an elephant was one of the tests of manhood for a young warrior.

But it was not only Somali adolescents who sought to prove themselves in this way. Rennie Bere tells of the exploit of Edward Omara, an Acholi of northern Uganda.

'. . . during a severe drought, a big bull took possession of the only usable water-hole in a considerable area. No-one could draw water and two women had been killed. The animal retired to impenetrable cover whenever danger threatened and several experienced rifle shots had failed to deal with it.

Then Edward sharpened his spears and went out to meet the challenge. He provoked a charge, stood his ground and killed the elephant with his spear. For this act of supreme courage, carried out in response to great public need, he was awarded the George Cross.'

Edward must have had great strength and very sharp spears thus to bring down a charging tusker. The main difficulty about facing an elephant with only primitive weapons is that of penetrating the animal's tough hide.

One way of surmounting this problem was to tip spears and arrows with poison. The Dorobo hunter-gatherers of the Mount Kenya forests were expert in the making of a most toxic substance from the leaves of the small Acocanthera tree. The leaves were boiled up in water for about six hours. Then the liquid was strained and reduced further until a thick, black, pitch-like substance was produced, which was spread on sheets of bark and kept until wanted. To keep the potent poison away from children and domestic animals it was always stored in the high fork of a tree. Neither the poison itself nor poisoned arrows were ever kept in the Dorobos' huts. These great hunters were so famed for their arrow poison that other people travelled long distances to buy it from them. The Dorobo hunted elephants with a short spear which he hurled from as short a range as possible to ensure maximum penetration. The poisoned tip of the spear was barbed and fixed to the shaft in such a way that it detached itself after impact and remained stuck in the elephant, discharging its poison into the bloodstream. Death was not immediate and, indeed, the victim sometimes survived so long and wandered so far after receiving his fatal wound that the hunter was unable to follow him. When the Dorobo spearman did make a successful kill his whole village would gather round the carcase and, after carefully cutting out and discarding the area round the poisoned wound, would gorge themselves on the rest of the elephant's flesh.

Another way of penetrating the elephant's thick hide was the falling spear trap, favoured by the Banyoro of Uganda and their neighbours. A spot would be selected on an elephant trail through wooded country. The hunters took with them a heavy iron spear and fixed the blunt end firmly into one end of a log about ten feet long and six inches in diameter. The whole contraption, when complete, weighed several hundredweight. It was then suspended above the track and a trip-line was attached to it. The first elephant to stumble along the path set off the trap and the massive spear plunged into its neck or smashed through its spinal chord. A variation of this trick was for the spear to be suspended in a tree over a favourite elephant resting place. The hunter would wait in the tree and attempt to judge when his prey was directly beneath it before cutting the rope and allowing the spear to fall.

Elaborate techniques such as this were not widespread over Africa. Most hunters went out in packs and hunted with spears, relying on defeating their foe by sheer weight of numbers. Means were found to corner or slow down the victims to make it easier for the men to use their spears. In the dry season they might set fire to the grass and thus stampede the elephants in the direction they wanted them to go. An animal frightened, exhausted and half-blinded by smoke was a comparatively easy target. The Karamojong of northern Uganda slowed their quarry down by using a wheel, a rope and a heavy log. The hubless wheel was buried in a shallow hole on the elephant track. One end of the rope was fixed round its rim in a running noose and the other end was fastened to the log. When the elephant sprang the trap the noose tightened round his leg, the log impeded his progress and he was an easy prey for the men with the spears.

In such comparatively simple combat did the men of Africa for generations pit themselves against the giants of plain and forest. They hunted only to fulfil their needs. They ate the elephants's meat. They made tools and weapons from his bones. They fashioned cloaks, belts and sandals from his skin. Only for his tusks did they have little or no use.

But the relationship between man and elephant during those long primeval epochs went beyond the simple conflict of hunter and hunted. Man and beast were two forms of the same life. This was expressed in mythology and religion. Elephants could change into men, and men into elephants. The Lulua of Central Africa still tell a story in which the human and the animal are confused. It is a story which illustrates well the ageless awe and fear felt for the elephant but also the close sense of affinity with him. It tells of a child who climbed a tree and saw four Kapumbu (elephants) approaching:

'The four elephants took their trunks off and took their tusks off. They took their skins off. The four Kapumbu were four men.

'Now came the last Kapumbu, the fifth. He lifted up his trunk and sniffed. He really was an elephant, and he said to the others who were really men, "I smell man." The others said: "We four have smelled nothing. Do not worry, there is no man here." The fifth Kapumbu took off his trunk and his tusks and his hide. He was a man too. The five Kapumbu made a fire. They cooked and ate a meal. Then they became, four of them, elephants, and went off into the bush.

'The fifth Kapumbu-man stayed behind, still as a man. He looked up and saw the child. He said: "I am your father, take heed of what I say. Never kill a Kapumbu! Do not shoot at one with an arrow! I am your father, your Kapumbu!"

'The fifth Kapumbu put on his trunk, his tusks and his hide, and went away. The child took a whistle and blew it. The four Kapumbu heard that and said: "There was a man there after all, and he is mocking us." The four Kapumbu came back and tried to kill the child. The fifth Kapumbu, who was his father, tried to save him. The child fled to his village, and the four Kapumbu ran after him. There were blacksmiths working at the bellows. The four Kapumbu asked them: "Have you seen the child?" "We saw him, he went into that house over there." The four Kapumbu went in and brought the child out. Now the fifth Kapumbu came up and said: "I warned you but you would not listen. I will have no more to do with you." The four Kapumbu killed the child. They took away his Mukishe (soul) and turned it into a Kapumbu.'

It is useless to sentimentalise about this 'natural' relationship between man and the greatest of the animals but it was, perhaps, healthier than the one which replaced it when strangers arrived in Africa—strangers who saw the elephant only as the carrier of gleaming crescents of valuable white gold.

2

'Large elephant teeth, in fact, are now rarely found except in India, the demands of luxury having exhausted all those in our part of the world.'

—Pliny (A.D. 77)

The Hunt is Up

Twenty-five thousand years ago a man sat in a cave in a region that men would one day call France. A fire burned in the cave's narrow entrance and around it were chunks of raw mammoth meat and discarded bone from a recent meal. By the light of the fire the man was working, brow wrinkled in concentration, eyes straining with the intricacy of his craft. He was scraping with a sharpened flint at a fragment of mammoth tusk. Around him were scattered the charms he had been carving most of the day—simple but recognisable representations of bulls and deer which would bring the hunters success if they carried them. But now he was fashioning something else—a woman with long, retted hair and deep-set haunting eyes. Another charm? Designed to bring him luck in his own particular chase? We shall never know. What we can say with certainty is that the *Venus of Landes* was carved with feeling.

Ever since Aurignacian man in Upper Palaeolithic Europe manufactured his charms, craftsmen the world over have been carving ivory with feeling. The ivory has come from a variety of animals—mammoth, elephant, walrus, hippopotamus, whale, wild pig—but it has always been in demand and demand has made it the most valuable organic substance next to pearl. The reason for this is not immediately obvious. Ivory has disadvantages in comparison with some other natural materials. It is of variable quality. It often cracks and warps badly It discolours easily and it can be eaten by rats and insects. Yet it is not necessary to answer in words the question, 'why is ivory so popular?' All the questioner need do is look at a Benin ceremonial mask, a Gothic triptych, a Renaissance figurine, a Kashmiri Buddha or a Japanese netsuke. The beautiful patination, the intricacy of carving to which the material lends itself, the strength combined with grace—these qualities speak for themselves.

Ivory is dentine, a substance formed in the teeth of most mammals. Elephant ivory is not necessarily the best quality dentine available. Hippopotamus teeth are made of dentine which is extremely fine grained and is more durable than elephant ivory. For their finest work the ancient Persians preferred the teeth of sperm whales, which they obtained from Phoenician merchants. The importance of elephant tusks lies in their size. Since the mammoth became extinct the elephant has become the only source of large quantities of workable ivory. Elephant tusks start as do all teeth, as small pegs of dentine covered by hard protective enamel. But in these two teeth the dentine continues to grow throughout life at the enormous rate of about $\frac{3}{4}$ lb.–1 lb. per year each. An elderly elephant therefore finishes with enormous tusks, often with the small patch of original enamel still carried at the tip. The tusks have to grow quickly because they are subject to considerable wear. An elephant uses his tusks for digging in the earth to grub up roots and for stripping the bark from trees. Were this not so a bull surviving his allotted three score years and ten would end up with tusks far too heavy to be carried. Just as most men and women are right handed so most elephants rely on one tusk more than the other, which is why it is very unusual to find a perfect pair of tusks on one animal. The quality of ivory varies with the different types of elephant. Indian tusks, as well as being smaller than African, are rather brittle and less easy to work. The forest elephant produces dense, hard ivory which has a good colour but is also inclined to be brittle. The ivory of the bush elephant is softer and more suitable for carving although it has a 'creamier' colour and a more fibrous texture.

All the great ancient civilisations of Asia and Europe prized elephant ivory. Combs, knife handles, carved figures and other items revealing a high degree of skill have been found in predynastic (e.g. before *c.* 3000 B.C.) Egyptian sites and there were ivory carving centres in Babylon at the same time.* The large numbers of ivory objects found in royal tombs indicate beyond doubt that articles made from elephant tusks were status symbols eagerly coveted by the wealthy. Stylistic similarities suggest that much of the carving was done by itinerant crafts-men, probably Phoenicians. Certainly ivory was an important trading commodity for the merchants of Tyre and Sidon. One is reminded, inevitably, of Masefield's evocative lines on the theme of early Mediterranean trade:

'Quinquireme of Nineveh from distant Ophir,
Rowing home to haven in sunny Palestine,
With a cargo of ivory,
And apes and peacocks,
Sandalwood, cedarwood, and sweet white wine.'

When King Solomon was building the temple at Jerusalem (*c.* 1000 B.C.) he had such a need for ivory and precious metals to adorn the great edifice that he entered into a special com-mercial treaty with King Hiram of Tyre, as we read in I Kings X, 22-3:

'For the King had at sea a navy of Tharshish with the navy of Hiram: once in three years came the navy of Tharshish, bringing gold, and silver, ivory, and apes, and peacocks.
'So King Solomon exceeded all the kings of the earth for riches and for wisdom.'

Further evidence of his wealth was Solomon's ivory throne which, we are told, 'had six steps, and at the back of the throne was a calf's head, and on each side of the seat were arm rests, and two lions standing beside the arm rests, while twelve lions stood there, one on each end of a step on the six steps.' The whole thing was overlaid with gold and 'the like of it was never made in any kingdom'. Not to be outdone, a later King, Ahab, constructed a palace, so heavily ornamented with ivory that it

---

* In this section I have drawn heavily on Professor H. H. Scullard's *The Elephant in the Greek and Roman World* (1974).

was called the ivory house. Ivory came to be synonymous with luxury and decadence in the Hebrew kingdom and as such was denounced by the eighth-century prophet, Amos:

'Woe to those who lie upon beds of ivory,
And stretch themselves upon their couches . . .
Who sing idle songs to the sound of the harp . . .
Who drink wine in bowls,
And anoint themselves with the finest oils,
But are not grieved over the ruins of Joseph.'

Ivory featured prominently in what was probably the most culturally advanced early Mediterranean civilisation—Minoan Crete. At the palace of Zacro, which is known to have been destroyed about 1450 B.C., archaeologists found four elephant tusks. At Kronos an ivory carver's workshop was unearthed in which there were still many traces of large statuettes and cylindrical caskets carved in relief. It was probably here that the technique later made famous by great Greek sculptors such as Phidias was perfected of facing large statues with plates of ivory, pinned together, and decorated with gold leaf. Some of the most beautiful and famous of all ivory artifacts were made in ancient Crete, such as the figures of acrobats now in the museum at Candia.

Little has survived of the ivory work of the early Classical period in Greece but we know from contemporary writings that large quantities of the material were used by the craftsmen of Athens, Sparta and other centres. The greatest artist of them all was Phidias who lived in the middle of the fifth century B.C. and to whom Pericles gave an important role in the rebuilding of Athens. His statue of Zeus for the temple at Olympia was one of the wonders of the ancient world. It certainly must have consumed prodigious amounts of ivory. The great seated figure was over forty feet high and was entirely overlaid with ivory, decorated in its turn with gold. Phidias also made a statue of Athena similar in size for the Parthenon.

Rome—powerful, acquisitive, Philisitine Rome—consumed ivory in great quantities, as she consumed everything which symbolised wealth and majesty. Republican and imperial officials used ivory for their staffs of office, insignia and curule chairs. Votive offerings of tusks adorned the temples. Cicero spoke of 'houses of marble that glitter with ivory and gold' and from the writers of every Roman century we learn that the substance was used for luxury items from furniture inlay to book-covers, from bird cages to brooches and from combs to scabbards. Seneca owned 500 tripod tables with ivory legs while some of the emperors displayed a profligacy in their use of ivory which showed a complete lack of understanding of the difficulties of supply. Caligula, not content with naming his horse a consul, gave the creature an ivory stable. The plundering of the elephant herds to provide wealthy Romans with luxuries continued unabated. It is surely significant that in the splendid mozaic villa floor unearthed at Piazza Armerina in Sicily a figure symbolising Africa carries as her sceptre an elephant tusk.

Where, then, did all this ivory come from? There were three main areas of supply; India, Syria and North Africa (including Egypt). The earliest Egyptian craftsmen were able to use the tusks of elephants which were native to their own country. Originally elephants were to be found throughout the entire continent even in places where today life is impossible for wild animals and difficult for man. 6,000 year old rock paintings of elephant can still be seen in the Eastern Desert and the Tibesti Hills, in the middle of the Sahara. Climatic changes drove the grassland back and with it its human and animal inhabitants. While some elephants retreated southwards others moved to the north and north-east, to the Nile valley and the Mediterranean littoral. But the dessication continued and around 3000 B.C. (between the First and Fourth Dynasties) the herds were gradually disappearing from Egypt. Two source areas of African elephants were left throughout Classical times; Ethiopia and the northern Sudan (and to some extent Somalia), and the Maghreb. The elephants who lived in these regions were almost certainly of the forest type (*cyclotis*). For hundreds of years ivory found its way down the commercial highway of the Nile to Thebes and Memphis. Occasionally expeditions were despatched southwards in search of tusks. One such was organised about 1500 B.C. by Queen Hatshepsut, who, inspired by religious zeal, was in the midst of an energetic temple building programme.

But the south could not produce enough ivory to meet Egypt's needs. The great rulers of the New Kingdom, Thutmose I and Thutmose III, invaded Syria, and one of their reasons for this extension of empire was their desire to secure a supply of ivory from the Syrian herds. We are told that on one expedition Thutmose III personally hunted and killed 120 elephants.

The Syrian elephants were related to the Indian species and it was they which had provided most of the tusks for the craftsmen of Phoenicia, Babylon and Assyria. They bore the brunt of the quest for ivory throughout much of the ancient period. As well as professional hunters, kings went on elephant *battues*. A stele of *c.* 879 records the boast of the Assyrian, Assurnasirpal II, that he had killed 450 lions, 200 ostriches and 30 elephants. Do these proportions, one wonders, reflect the relative scarcity of elephants or the king's lack of skill in hunting them? Ivory figured prominently in the tribute paid by vassal states to their overlords and in the booty obtained from defeated capitals. The uncontrolled activities of the hunters gradually and inevitably thinned out the Syrian herds. By 500 B.C. there were no wild elephants left in the Middle East.

By then the Phoenicians had long since discovered another source of ivory. The colonists of Carthage found elephants in the Atlas mountains and exploited them to the full. From Asia they brought the techniques of training elephants as beasts of burden and war machines. The mighty creatures played an important part in the economic and military life of North Africa and in the city of Carthage there was stabling for 600 elephants. Their finest hour—and perhaps the finest hour of all domesticated elephants—came in 218 B.C. when 37 of them went with Carthage's greatest son, Hannibal, through Spain and France then crossed the Alps to inflict upon great Rome the worst defeat she ever suffered on her own territory. But the majority of North Africa's elephants did not find such honourable employment; they were ruthlessly exploited for their ivory by Carthaginians and, later, by Romans. The result was inevitable; the herds of North Africa followed those of Syria into extinction. By the end of the fourth century A.D. there were no more elephants north of the Sahara. Nor was this the last region of Africa to be denuded of its elephant population by human pressures.

Beyond the desert the vast herds of the forest and plains were safe and so they remained for a few centuries. Few Africans hunted for ivory, though the craftsmen of Benin and other states on the middle and lower Niger developed great skill as workers of ivory, producing beautifully carved masks, statuettes, caskets, jewellery, bells, rattles and emblems of office. Then, in the seventh and eighth centuries, the Muslim Arab invasion swept across North Africa. As soon as the conquerors had established themselves they sought to open up commercial relations with the peoples south of the Sahara for they knew that in those distant lands there were commodities which the rest of the world prized highly—gold and ivory. Camel caravans were soon venturing into the wilderness of sand beyond Fez and Marrakesh and, by 1000 A.D. regular trading connections had been established with the peoples of the western Sudan. African towns like Kumbi Saleh, Timbuktu and Gao mushroomed into commercial entrepôts where Africans exchanged elephant tusks for salt from the desert mines at Taghaza and exotic novelties such as silk, copper ornaments, damascened swords, pots and pans.

On the other side of the continent the peoples of East Africa were slowly extending their overseas contacts. From time immemorial the coast had been on the fringe of the vigorous Indian Ocean trade system. A second-century Alexandrian Greek described the commercial life of the East African coast thus:

'There are imported into these markets the lances made at Mocha [in Arabia] especially for this trade, and hatchets and daggers and awls, and various kinds of glass; and at some places a little wine and wheat, not for trade but to serve for getting the goodwill of the savages. There are exported from these places a great deal of ivory, but inferior to that of Adulis [India], and rhinoceros—horn and tortoiseshell . . . and a little palm oil.'

The quest for ivory which had taken the merchants of Egypt on occasional visits to the Red Sea ports impelled the traders of Arabia and the Persian Gulf to explore the coastline further south. They were aided by the monsoon winds which blew their lateen-sailed dhows south-westwards between November and April, then obligingly turned round to blow them home again between May and October. The Arabs did not find the 'people of Zenj' (i.e. the black people) the best of trading partners. Though they were eager enough to do business and would cheerfully barter ivory for iron goods, cowries and cheap cloth, they could not ensure a regular supply of tusks. Everything depended on the skill and luck of the hunters who pursued the herds living in the immediate vicinity of the coast. The traders could never obtain enough ivory and most of what they did buy went to India and China, as the tenth-century writer Al-Masudi records:

'Although constantly employed in hunting elephants and gathering ivory, the Zenj make no use of ivory for their own domestic purposes. They wear iron instead of gold and silver . . . Tusks go generally to Oman, and from there are sent on to China and India. That is the route they follow, and were it otherwise, ivory would be very abundant in Muslim countries. In China the kings and their military and civilian officers use carrying-chairs of ivory; no official or person of rank would dare to visit the king in an iron chair, and ivory alone is used for this purpose . . . Ivory is much prized in India; there it is made into handles for the daggers known as *harari* or *harri* in the singular, as well as for the hilts of curved swords . . . But the biggest use of ivory is in the manufacture of chessmen and other gaming pieces.'

It is almost certain that al-Masudi was not quite correct in his assessment of the uses of ivory; the most important use for the substance in India has always been the manufacture of marriage bangles for Hindu women. African tusks were better for this purpose because, being of a greater diameter than Indian tusks, they provided more bangles. It is interesting to note that during the Middle Ages the greatest demand for ivory was in those countries which had the longest history of craftsmanship using native ivory. India had its own elephants; in China the supply of ivory from long-buried mammoths lasted for a surprisingly long time. As these sources began to dwindle carvers and merchants welcomed the ivory which came from the Land of Zenj.

It was probably the need to create a more reliable trading system which led some of the Arab merchants to set up colonies on the coasts and islands of East Africa. This process had already begun by 1000 A.D. Al-Masudi tells us that there were Muslims living on the island of Qanbalu (Pemba), and that is unlikely to have been the only settlement. The unknown territories of the African interior and the deliberate policies of coastal chiefs restricted the foreigners to their walled towns, although by the mid-fifteenth century Arab boats had penetrated far up the Zambezi from their base at Sofala to buy ivory from the Tonga and the Lenje. Recent research has revealed how, over the years, a complex network of long-distance trade built up, involving many African communities by means of which ivory, copper, gold and other products of the interior reached the foreign buyers at the coast. Beads and cowries have been found at grave sites far inland and bespeak a flourishing Afro-Arab commerce.

What little ivory reached medieval Europe did so by courtesy of the Muslim world. By way of the trans-Saharan routes and the Red Sea, tusks reached the entrepôts of Tunis, Ceuta, Alexandria and Syrian Tripoli, to be ferried across the Mediterranean by the galleys of Constantinople, Venice and Genoa. It was the desire to find a back door to this trade which first inspired Portuguese adventurers to explore the Atlantic seaboard of the unknown continent. Henry 'the Navigator', fourth son of John I of Portugal and prime mover in this daring experiment, hoped to find a new seaway to India and Cathay but if that dream were not realised at least it should prove possible to establish commercial links with the African world which would be independent of the cursed Muslims.

League by league Henry's mariners edged their flimsy ships along the barren coast of West Africa. It was not until some years after the Navigator's death in 1460 that they reached a land where ivory was to be found in abundance. They called it Ivory Coast. By the first decade of the sixteenth century the Portuguese had completed their exploration of the African coast, had marked out the places ripe for exploitation, had established bases and built forts. Some African rulers, such as the Manikongo of the lower Congo region, became clients (and soon vassals). The Muslim rulers of East Africa were simply elbowed out of the white man's way as he muscled in on their trade. Spurred by the demands of a vital continent just awakening to the fabled riches of unexplored areas the new conquerors stimulated fresh life on the old trade routes to the interior. African traders brought unprecedented quantities of ivory to Luanda, Banguela, Mozambique and Mombasa. More and more African rulers were drawn into the commercial network and assumed the role of middle men, trading in copper, slaves, palm oil and salt, as well as ivory. For many years the tusks of freshly killed elephants were augmented by the supplies of 'found' ivory which had lain in the undergrowth for years or been used as stockade posts. An English visitor to Angola in the seventeenth century reported seeing great piles of tusks awaiting transportation by the merchants. In the sixteenth century 30,000 lbs. of ivory passed annually through the port of Sofala.

But Portugal's resources were slender and over-extended. By the middle of the seventeenth century European rivals had stripped her of most of her bases on the Guinea coast. A successful Arab revolt in 1696–8 drove the Portuguese from the east coast north of Cape Delgado. Africa's first colonial power clung precariously, though successfully, to her footholds in Angola and Mozambique until recent times but for over two centuries she did little more than cling on.

The ivory trade continued and, in the nineteenth century, there occurred an expansion of this difficult commerce which can only be adequately described as an explosion. There were two main reasons for this: a well-organised supply and an unprecedented demand. The demand was created by the industrial 'nouveau riche' of Europe and America. Like the acquisitive élite of Roman society, the new Philistines demanded that every kind of tawdry luxury the world could provide should be brought to their door. This included artifacts of ivory—keys for the piano without which no Victorian drawing-room was complete, balls for the newly-fashionable game of billiards, fans for use in stuffy ballrooms, card cases, letter openers, buttons and a host of unnecessary but desirable knick-knacks.

As for the supply, this was organised by the traditional African entrepreneurs and the Muslims of Arabia and Egypt. By 1800 the principal trade routes to the interior were well established. Yao, Nyamwezi, Bisa, Kasanje, Matamba and other traditional experts were making regular long journeys to convey ivory to the ports. But the supply was still inadequate to meet the international demand and so the coastal traders for the first time ventured inland. Armed with guns and large parties of armed followers and spurred on by the vast profits to be made, they trod for themselves the old trails through forest and scrubland.

It was Said ibn Sultan, ruler of Oman, who organised the new onslaught. The departure of the Portuguese from East Africa had left the way open for the rulers of Oman to claim dominion. Said was the man who, at length, made good that claim. By 1832 he had established control of all the Arab settlements and, in 1840, to underline that control he moved his capital from hot, arid Muscat to the island of Zanzibar. There, and on the neighbouring island of Pemba, he laid the foundations of the clove industry which was to become the basis of his successors' prosperity. He established diplomatic relations with all the leading nations of the western world and invited them to trade in his newly improved harbour at Zanzibar. It was to provide slaves for his plantations and ivory for his trading partners that Said despatched caravans to the interior and made treaties with powerful chiefs hundreds of miles inland. What Said did at Zanzibar, Muhammad Ali, ruler of Egypt, did at Cairo. By the middle of the nineteenth century armies of ivory and slave traders were advancing from the north and the east towards the very centre of Africa.

The results were more appalling than words can describe. Ivory lust and contempt for human life made the second half of the nineteenth century the blackest and bloodiest epoch in the long history of a turbulent continent. The merchants who trekked the caravan routes, toiled up the rivers, hacked into the forests and penetrated every year further into the core of Africa were obsessed by one thought—to amass as much ivory as possible and convey it as cheaply as possible to the coast. They staked life and fortune on their ventures to the interior and for that reason they could allow nothing and no one to stand between them and the successful accomplishment of their desperate missions. Commerce in slaves became inextricably entwined with the ivory trade. There was scarcely a European traveller who entered the continent from the east or north who failed to report with horror on the manacled gangs of captives stumbling along under the weight of immense tusks and perpetually 'encouraged' by the whips of their overseers.

A. J. Swann, a technical agent with the London Missionary Society, though he had heard many tales about the trade was nevertheless quite unprepared for the full horror of the first slave caravan he encountered:

'As they filed past we noticed many chained together by the neck. Others had their necks fastened into the forks of poles about 6 feet long, the ends of which were supported by the men who preceded them.* The women, who were as numerous as the men, carried babies on their backs in addition to a tusk of ivory or other burden on their heads. . . .

'It is difficult adequately to describe the filthy state of their bodies; in many instances not only scarred by the cut of a "chikote" (a piece of hide used to enforce obedience), but feet and shoulders were a mass of open sores, made more painful by the swarms of flies which followed the march and lived on the flowing blood. They presented a moving picture of utter misery, and one could not help wondering how many of them had survived the long tramp from the Upper Congo, at least 1000 miles distant. Our own inconveniences sank into insignificance compared with the suffering of this crowd of half-starved, ill-treated creatures who, weary and friendless, must have longed for death.

'The head-men in charge were most polite to us as they passed our camp. Each was armed with a rifle, knife and spear, and although decently clothed in clean cotton garments, they presented a thoroughly villainous appearance.

'Addressing one, I pointed out that many of the slaves were unfit to carry loads. To this he smilingly replied:

' "They have no choice! *They must go or die!*"

---

* This forked pole was the infamous taming-stick or 'gorree'. The slave's neck was held fast by a metal bar across the two prongs of the fork. Apart from the discomfort involved, the bar was so fixed that if the wretched man struggled or even stumbled badly he risked breaking his neck.

'Then ensued the following conversation:—

' "Are all these slaves destined for Zanzibar?"

' "Most of them, the remainder will stay at the coast."

' "Have you lost many on the road?"

' "Yes, numbers have died of hunger!"

' "Any run away?"

' "No, they are too well guarded. Only those which become possessed with the devil try to escape: there is nowhere they could run to if they should go."

' "What do you do when they become too ill to travel?"

' "Spear them at once!" was the fiendish reply. "For if we did not others would pretend that they were ill in order to avoid carrying their loads! No! we never leave them alive on the road; they all know our custom."

' "I see women carrying not only a child on their backs, but, in addition, a tusk of ivory or other burden on their heads. What do you do in their case when they become too weak to carry both child and ivory? Who carries the ivory?"

' "She does! We cannot leave valuable ivory on the road. *We spear the child and make her burden lighter*. Ivory first, child afterwards!" '

Swann was dumbfounded by such open and brazen villainy. He comments, in true Thomas Hughes style, 'I could have struck the demon dead at my feet.'

Negroes and elephant tusks; both torn with agony from the life of Africa; both destined for sale to foreigners. It took little ingenuity for an early observer to coin the phrase 'black and white ivory'. And yet that phrase, implying as it does a straightforward connection between the two trades is, like most catch-phrases, too simple. It suggests that slaves and ivory were of equal importance; that it was desire for both commodities which drove coastal traders into inland Africa. In reality, the main preoccupation of the merchants was always ivory; slaves were a nuisance and they were expendable. Only this can explain the wanton brutality with which they were treated and which so puzzled European observers like Livingstone:

'One woman had her infant's brain knocked out, because

she could not carry her load and it; and a man was despatched with an axe because he had broken down with fatigue . . . in this traffic we increasingly find self-interest overcome by contempt of human life and bloodthirstiness.'

The missionaries always had the appalling horrors of the slave trade in the forefront of their vision. To them the needless killing of slaves appeared not only as utter barbarity but also as inexplicably bad business. Why go to all the trouble of capturing slaves and then murder them by neglect or brutality before they reached the coastal markets? In reality, what mattered to the Arabs was getting their precious load of ivory to the coast. The slaves which survived the journey and could thus be sold at Zanzibar constituted a bonus profit but their importance to the expedition was marginal.

Throughout that extensive part of Africa which fed the east coast markets the period from 1850 to 1890 was the heyday of the Zanzibaris, the white-robed, turbaned Arab and half-caste merchants who made such a mixed impression on westerners who met them in their own inland haunts. They were reported to be effusive in their hospitality, fathomless in their treachery, precise and particular in displays of courtesy, wanton and profligate in exhibitions of needless brutality, brave adventurers, cowardly bullies, to outward appearances more civilised than the Africans among whom they lived but in their utter contempt for human life betraying a savagery which was none the less savage for being openly acknowledged. Even the most determined opponents of the slave trade could not fail to admit a reluctant admiration of the Zanzibaris. S. L. Hinde, who was in the Congo from 1891 to 1894 reported to the Royal Geographical Society on his return:

'Despite their slave-raiding propensities during the forty years of their domination, the Arabs have converted the Manyema and Malela country into one of the most prosperous in Central Africa. The landscape as seen from the hills in the neighbourhood of Nyangwe and Kasongo, reminds one strongly of an ordinary English arable country.'

In Ujiji, A. J. Swann was most forcibly struck by what his Anglo-Saxon mind could only conceive as a paradox:

'At this powerful centre of trade we were nothing less than guests of the Arabs. Mighty merchant princes who lived in a curious mixture of luxury and squalor, invited us to tiffin. One walked over tusks of ivory scattered about their court-yards representing thousands of pounds. Diseased slaves moved about in close proximity to gaudily clothed women of the household. The slave-chain and its captives were in evidence everywhere, whilst brutal half-caste fighting men lounged about the verandahs of the most wealthy. The whole appearance of the place was like a whited sepulchre, presided over by smoothing-talking, clean, perfumed, and polite Arabs, who, in their conduct towards us, were always courteous and generous.'

The Arabs (they all preferred to be called Arabs, though most of them derived from mixed marriages) had established them-selves in their inland centres as comfortably and as arrogantly as any contemporary British officers in their garrisons on the Indian frontier. Tabora, Ujiji, Kasongo and Nyangwe had become Arab towns defended from intrusion as much by an aura of cultural superiority as by walls and guns. Throughout history the Arab has always loved to travel. Wherever he has wandered he has carried with him his hardy, transplantable culture, which has taken root and flourished, sometimes in the most unlikely ground. Beside simple African villages in the burnt and sprawling plain appeared suburbs of wooden and stone houses, neatly laid-out gardens and groves, shaded walks and carpeted verandahs, H. M. Stanley discovered when he made his trans-continental journey between 1874 and 1876:

'There are many who are in better circumstances in the interior than they would be on their own island of Zanzibar. Some of them have hundreds of slaves, and he would be a poor Arab indeed who possessed only ten. These slaves, under their masters' direction, have constructed roomy, comfortable, flat-roofed houses, or lofty, cool huts, which, in the dangerous and hostile districts, are surrounded by strong stockades. Thus, at Unyanyembe [Tabora] there are sixty or seventy large stockades enclosing the owner's house and store-rooms, as well as the numerous huts of his slaves. Ujiji, again, may be described as a long, straggling village, formed by the large tembes of the Arabs; and Nyangwe is another settlement similar to Ujiji. Many of the Arabs settled in the pastoral districts possess large herds of cattle and extensive fields where rice, wheat, Indian corn, and millet are cultivated, besides sugar-cane and onions, and the fruit trees of Zanzibar —the orange, lemon, pawpaw, mango and pomegranate—now being gradually introduced.'

The wealthiest of these inland Zanzibaris lived in fine style indeed, their wants ministered to by servants, harem women and armies of slaves. A. J. Swann's account of a nocturnal visit to Rumaliza, leader of the Ujiji traders, reads like something out of the Arabian Nights:

'Entering a large courtyard, I was conducted along corridors dimly lighted by small palm-oil lamps. Not a soul was about but ourselves. Passing through a beautifully carved entrance, the door of which opened as we approached, although no-one was visible to me, I knew that we had entered the outer division of his harem, as the messenger closed the door, saying: "I must return! Wait where you are until someone comes. When I have closed the door, give the usual salutation. I must not see the women, good-bye!"

'A small lamp was suspended from the low roof, and a second was half hidden in a recesss at the extreme end of the room. There was no furniture, nothing but a beautifully-worked, coloured praying mat hung on the wall. I recognised at once that I was standing in the private room where the master performed his devotions. "Hodi! Hodi!" I exclaimed...

'A soft female voice replied:

' "Hodini! hodini! Karibu, bwana!" ("Come in, sir: you are welcome.")

'With a light step, a beautiful young girl, about fifteen years of age, approached, clad in rich clothes thrown gracefully over her shoulders. The draught carried towards me a delicious perfume, of which these Eastern women are fond.

' "Twenda, bwana!" ("Let us go together") she said, moving towards the interior of the house.

'I followed through three small rooms into a well-furnished

apartment. Here the girl beckoned to me to be seated on the sofa, saying: "Master will be with you at once; he is having his bath."

'I was not kept waiting many minutes, for Rumaliza came in quickly, leaving his sandals outside, and with a smile held out his hand, giving me the usual Arab welcome.

'A lovely woman brought a bowl of water for me to wash my hands, another sprinkled scent over my handkerchief, a third placed hot coffee and cakes at our feet, which we partook of in Eastern fashion . . .

'The meal was soon over, the scented, dark damsels were called to remove the utensils, and as they passed out, handed us a light fan to keep away mosquitoes. It was very picturesque, quiet, clean, Oriental, and, in its way, fascinating.'

The Arabs settled inland, sometimes permanently, sometimes for a few years at a stretch. They traded in their own right or acted as agents for wealthy principals. They provided valuable services to passing caravans as purveyors of trade goods and information, as negotiators with local rulers and as hirers of ivory porters. They had all come into the interior as ivory traders but they stayed in the interior for a variety of reasons. Some simply found the life more congenial. At Tabora or Ujiji a man with a few slaves, some guns and a little capital was a person of consequence. Life there was more luxurious and hedged about with fewer restrictions than life at the coast. Some had failed in their trading ventures and did not dare to return to face their creditors in the law courts of Zanzibar. Yet others were fugitives from the Sultan's justice, who found in the wide expanses of Africa a spacious sanctuary and an arena where vicious and criminal acts did not transgress the law of the bush. But the Arabs were not the only men who entered nineteenth-century Africa in pursuit of ivory. The white hunter was about to make his appearance.

3

'Are you not afraid,' said he, *'so thinly attended, to venture upon these long and dangerous voyages?'*
'. . . my servants are indeed few, but they are veteran soldiers, tried and exercised from their infancy in arms, and I value not the superior number of cowardly and disorderly persons.'

—James Bruce, TRAVELS TO DISCOVER THE
SOURCE OF THE NILE (1790)

Into the Dark Continent

1942552

It was during the middle months of 1837—at about the same time that England was celebrating the accession of an eighteen-year-old queen—that Captain William Cornwallis Harris of the Honourable East India Company's Engineers wrote an account of the first hunting expedition into the interior of southern Africa. Harris, a young officer on sick leave from India, was the first white man to travel far beyond the frontiers of European settlement in Africa solely for sport. He was followed by an increasing number of enthusiasts throughout the nineteenth century and well into the twentieth. But the majority of these hunters made their journeys after 1885 when Africa—on paper at least—had been divided up into European colonies. The pioneers of the previous fifty years were venturing into unknown, unmapped regions. In a very real sense they were on a par with the pioneer missionaries. They were not, perhaps, as selfless and altruistic as the heralds of the Christian gospel but they were drawn into the wild remoteness of an unknown continent by a missionary passion to see and record its human and animal life.

Nineteenth-century European society had little room for eccentrics. Men who would not employ themselves in honest commerce or in discharging their duties as landowners were an embarrassment. There was only one accepted career open to restless young men—the army. But even that held little interest

35

for those who had a real lust for action and excitement. Apart from the Crimean fiasco Europe experienced no serious military engagements between 1815 and 1871. India and Africa provided opportunities for occasional campaigns against ill-armed natives, but what was that to young men who thought of war as a glorious and honourable pastime, a superior game played by dashing heroes in gorgeous costumes on well-bred chargers? The more high spirited broke the chains of frustration and pursued the holy grail of adventure wherever it led. It led some to Africa.

Roualeyn George Gordon Cumming, a second son of a Scottish baronet, pursued a career entirely appropriate to a young man of aristocratic origins—Eton, a commission in the East India Company's Madras Cavalry, followed by early retirement for health reasons to his Scottish estates. But at the age of twenty-one he craved real adventure, esteeming 'the life of the wild hunter so far preferable to that of the mere sportsman'. He undertook further military service in Canada and South Africa. Then resigned his commission, bought a wagon, essential supplies, hired a few porters and became one of the pioneer hunter-explorers in Southern Africa.

John Boyes ran away from his home in Hull at the age of fifteen. He went to sea, spent five years travelling the oceans in various vessels and eventually fetched up in Durban. He worked his way around South Africa doing a variety of jobs—baker, locomotive fireman, policeman, mule-driver, grocer, actor and deck hand on an Arab dhow. This last occupation took him to Mombasa on the east coast and from there he made his way to the Kikuyu country south of Mount Kenya. From this base he began a career as an ivory hunter which was to last many years and take him far into the interior.

R. J. Cunninghame was another adventurer who eventually arrived in East Africa. His earlier career included whaling in the Antarctic and driving a mail coach. When he reached the Kenya Highlands he was clad in little more than a blue sweater and a long beard. Yet he was to become one of the first and most successful professional hunters and was employed by many wealthy clients as a safari leader. He won a D.S.O. in the 1914–18 war.

William Cotton Oswell went to India as an agent of the East

India Company, but won more acclaim as a hunter than in the prosecution of his official duties. It was ill health that first took him to Africa in 1847, but to judge from his record he was hampered very little by weakness or infirmity. His tenacity and skill as a hunter earned him the nickname of the 'Nimrod of South Africa' and he was also a pioneer explorer. For instance he crossed the Kalahari with Livingstone to discover Lake Ngami and he was at the great missionary's side again when Livingstone reached the Zambezi. His thirst for adventure subsequently took him to the Crimean War, and to some of the remoter parts of North and South America.

Paul Du Chaillu was the son of a wealthy French merchant who traded in Africa. The fact that his father died young, probably of fever contracted on the West African coast did not deter the young man from becoming the first European to penetrate deep into the Equatorial forest. At the age of twenty-five he organised in America an expedition to the Gatson River. He devoted the next ten years to hunting, exploring and making notes on the flora and fauna of Central Africa. Nor were his adventuring days over. Later expeditions took him far north to the remoter parts of Scandinavia. He was still on his travels when he died in St. Petersburg at the age of seventy-two.

Walter Bell (Karamoja Bell as he was later to be known) relates that Africa had got its hooks into him while he was still at prep school:

> 'As time rolled on I became more and more convinced that I had somehow got on the wrong road. School seemed to my muddled brain to lead nowhere near to the dazzling visions of sunlit prairies filled with pasturing herds of elephants waiting for my deadly rifle to lay them out. I formed the determination to end it all and get out, and so I just left for home. When asked by my guardian what I was going to do, I said I was going to Africa to hunt elephants.'

Bell's guardians tried to do their best for him by sending him to sea. When that experiment failed the troublesome young man was enrolled in a German 'crammer' to catch up on his education. This Teutonic academy could not hold Bell long. He affected a dramatic escape by canoe. Finally, when he was seventeen, his elders and betters gave way to Bell's demands to be allowed to go to Africa. They probably hoped profoundly that his experiences there would prove fatal.

F. C. Selous, one of the most famous elephant hunters, went to Africa at the age of twenty and spent the rest of his life there, hunting, trading, fighting in the Ndebele War and leading official safaris. At the age of sixty he insisted on taking part in the East African campaigns of the First World War and entered upon the new 'adventure' with as much fervour as he had displayed in all his earlier escapades. He regularly marched his subordinates into the ground and allowed no concessions to be made to his advanced years. He was killed on active service in Tanganyika.

Such were the men of pioneering generations of African hunters. They were extravagant, larger-than-life characters who were usually quite misunderstood by their own contemporaries, both white and black. Du Chaillou's reception by the Mpongure of the equatorial coast was fairly typical of the attitude of Africans towards white adventurers:

'I was obliged to inform them that I had come . . . to explore the country, of which I heard so many wonderful stories from them, and to hunt wild birds and beasts.

'At first they believed I was joking. When they saw landed from the vessels which brought me no "trade", but only an outfit of all things necessary for a hunter's life in the African wilds, they began perforce to believe in my stated purpose. Then their amazement and perplexity knew no bounds.

'Some thought I was out of my senses and pitied my father, whom they all knew, for being troubled with such a good-for-nothing son . . . They surrounded me, each with his tale of the horrors and dangers of a voyage "up the country", asserting that I should be eaten up by cannibals, drowned in rivers, devoured by tigers (*sic*) and crocodiles, crushed by elephants, upset by hippopotomi, or waylaid and torn to pieces by the gorilla.'

The motivation of an African hunter was not the easiest to

understand. Probably James Sutherland expressed it most clearly:

'To all intents and purposes we are absolutely free; there is no vexatious etiquette to be observed; I can burst into a hearty laugh without shocking the ridiculous propriety of a crowded street; I do not require to wear this kind of waistcoat or that kind of tie. The morning coat and silk hat I wore on my last brief visit to England, I flung into the sea in sheer exuberance of spirits, when I left Marseilles glad to be quit of costly insanity—even a bowler hat is a ludicrous menace to my sense of natural comfort. Alas! though the pari (forest) is a place where life is action, it gives a man a great deal of time to think: it focuses his view; it peels from his mind the trivial veneer of civilization and leaves him to brood upon the elemental things which lie at the heart of life. There is also something wistful, tender and infinitely beautiful that forms an undercurrent to the magnificent heedlessness of the wild. It calls and calls.'

The pioneer white hunters worked their way inland from established areas of European settlement. Most of them began their travels in South-East Africa. Few areas of the world can have been in as disturbed a state as was South-East Africa in the first half of the last century. It was the scene of some of the last great mass migrations and population clashes. For centuries Bantu peoples had been drifting southwards driving before them the earlier hunting-herding inhabitants usually known as Bushmen and Hottentots.* But by about 1800 the Bantu vanguard met up with a people who were less easily displaced. They had reached the frontier of Cape Colony. The results were catastrophic. In the region of the Great Fish River the border conflicts between the Xhosa and the Boers known as the Kaffir Wars spanned a violent century. Further inland the checking of the Bantu surge led to the *Mfecane*—the Time of Troubles. Competition for farmland and pasture drove the Africans to ever fiercer warfare among themselves. Then in 1818 the great Zulu chief Shaka launched his highly trained *impis* against his

---

* These groups are more correctly known by their linguistic appelation—i.e. San and Khoikhoi.

neighbours. No-one could stand up to the fearsome bravery and technical skill of the Zulus. Dispossessed chiefs could only lead their peoples and their cattle in search of new lands and launch their warriors against weaker settlements. The Time of Troubles was a chain reaction of violence. It threw up great warrior chiefs like Mzilikaze of the Ndebele and Moshweshwe of the Basuto. It plunged large areas of eastern and central Africa into chaos as desperate hordes raided, looted, foraged and murdered over thousands of miles.

Meanwhile further south another desperate horde was on the move. In 1836 many of the Boers, unable to endure the British yoke and contemptuous of a people who placed black men 'on an equal footing with Christians, contrary to the laws of God, and the natural distinction of race and colour' began the Great Trek which was to result in appalling hardship, frequent clashes with the Africans they wished to dispossess and violent death for many.

These disturbances inevitably had their effect on the wild life of South Africa, and particularly on the elephant population. During a period of some forty years these animals disappeared with astonishing rapidity and completeness from areas where vast herds had roamed for centuries. About 1820 elephant were to be seen close to the south-east coast and along the banks of the Fish, Kei and Buffalo rivers. Sixteen years later William Harris had to wait until he reached the Magaliesberg Hills, some five hundred miles inland (near modern Pretoria), for his first sight of elephants. When he did find them, though, he found them in abundance:

'. . . a grand and magnificent panorama was before us, which beggars all description. The whole face of the landscape was actually covered with wild Elephants. There could not have been fewer than three hundred within the scope of our vision. Every height and green knoll was dotted over with groups of them, whilst the bottom of the glen exhibited a dense and sable living mass—their colossal forms being at one moment partially concealed by the trees which they were disfiguring with giant strength; and at others seen emerging majestically into the open glades, bearing in their trunks the branches of trees with which they indolently protected themselves from the flies. The background was filled by a limited peep of the blue mountainous range, which here assumed a remarkably precipitous character, and completed a picture at once soul-stirring and sublime!'

For some years hunters had good sport among elephant herds in the western Transvaal but by the late 1850s William Baldwin was reporting that the best elephant shooting was to be had four hundred miles north beyond the Limpopo. By 1870 the situation had changed again, as Selous wrote:

'In those districts of Southern Africa . . . where . . . every species of wild game native to that part of the world, from the ponderous elephant to the graceful springbuck, was to be met with in such surprising numbers that vast tracts of country assumed the appearance of huge zoological gardens, one may now travel for days without seeing a single wild animal. In British Bechuanaland the elephant and rhinoceros are as extinct as the mammoth in England.'

It was obviously not only the Boers and the Bantu who were on the move.

There were reasons other than the troubled condition of human society for the thinning out and migration of the elephant herds. In part this phenomenon was an exaggerated manifestation of the normal pattern of elephant behaviour. These vast, destructive creatures are always on the move, demolishing their habitat and moving on—literally—to 'fresh fields and pastures new'. But that cannot of itself explain the almost total disappearance of the elephant from South Africa.

The answer is, once again, ivory. Some of the peoples of South Africa (e.g. the Pondo and the Tswana) were adept at elephant hunting but, as in other parts of the continent, they only killed for meat and their activities made no serious impression on the herds. When, however, they learned that white men would pay for tusks with guns, cloth and other desirables, their attitude changed dramatically; as Livingstone wrote in a letter on 17th October 1851:

'That Christian merchants who may have enterprise enough

to commence a trade in these parts would be no losers in the end may be inferred from what has taken place on this river (the Zouga) since its discovery. There being formerly no market, we saw many instances of ivory rotting in the sun. The people called the tusks "marapo hela", "bones only", and they shared the fate of other bones. Indeed they were much more anxious to sell a tusk worth in Graham's Town 4/6 per lb. than to part with a goat for a larger price, the whole value of which was not more than 2/6. We know of *900 elephants having been killed* on its banks since that period, and independently of quantities of ivory which have found their way to the Colony by other channels. A merchant at Kuruman took *23,000 lbs* of that article thither during the present year, and the greater portion of it came from this river alone.' (My emphases.)

In the troubled times of the *Mfecane* the appearance of the white hunter and trader was a godsend to many African chiefs. By offering him useless tusks they could obtain in return guns which were becoming vital for defence and conquest.

Boer traders also took their toll of the elephant population but excellent shots though they were, they were hampered by inadequate weapons when tackling the king of beasts. Until the early years of the nineteenth century many of them were still using antiquated match-lock and wheel-lock muskets. Then they started using the mammoth *roer*. This terrifying weapon was a 16-lb. muzzle loader primed with seventeen drams of powder and firing $\frac{1}{4}$-lb. balls. The explosion and recoil were enormous but, in the hands of an expert, this weapon was effective against elephants.

As well as African and Boer hunters there were the visiting sportsmen. William Cornwallis Harris was, as we have said, the first man to organise a shooting expedition to the interior. Having got together a group of Khoikhoi porters and guides he next invested in horses, oxcarts and hunting dogs and was soon ready to trek inland. It was in September 1836 that he left Graaff Reinet, 'the last outpost of civilisation' to cross the barren plateau beyond. For weeks their journey lay northwards through yellow-brown sameness, strewn with rocks and sickly vegetation. Their companions were the restless creatures of the veldt—wandering herds of gnu and springbok and the San hunters (Bushmen) who followed them from waterhole to waterhole.

Harris bagged a variety of animals whose skins and heads were added to his collection of trophies, but he had no sight of elephant. At Kuruman, an outpost of the London Missionary Society, he stayed as guest of the Reverend and Mrs Robert Moffat. Over the years many wanderers in South Africa were to be grateful for the hospitality of these famous pioneers and their still more famous son-in-law, David Livingstone. From Kuruman, Harris trekked north-eastwards, sighting and shooting many animals—but still finding no elephants. He passed through the territory of the feared Ndebele and their notorious leader, Mzilikaze, and at last reached the elephant country of the western Transvaal.

When he found his first small herd the elated Harris could think of nothing but getting in amongst them and making a kill:

'The group consisted of nine, all females with large tusks. We selected the finest, and with deliberation fired a volley of five balls into her. She stumbled, but recovering herself, uttered a shrill note of lamentation, when the whole party threw their trunks above their heads, and instantly clambered up the adjacent hill with incredible celerity. . . . We instantly mounted our horses, and the sharp loose stones not suiting the wounded lady, soon closed with her. Streaming with blood, and infuriated with rage, she turned upon us with uplifted trunk, and it was not until after repeated discharges, that a bael took effect in her brain, and threw her lifeless on the earth, which resounded with the fall.'

This indiscriminate and haphazard method of slaughter was characteristic of many of the early hunters. They knew little of elephant anatomy and even had they known, their guns would seldom have been equal to the task of bringing down an animal with a single, well-placed shot. Their circumstances dictated their technique. They had to hunt on horseback in order to keep up with their quarry, peppering it with repeated wounding shots until it dropped from exhaustion or loss of blood. Gordon Cumming once expended fifty-seven bullets in despatching one large bull. Inevitably many elephants escaped wounded into the forests to die a lingering death, their ivory lost to the hunter. The shooting of females in large numbers must have contributed considerably to the decimation of the herds. Harris, himself, robbed several baby elephants of their mothers.

Ignorant of the need for conservation, Harris was transported to the hunter's seventh heaven at having reached elephant country:

'. . . I felt my most sanguine expectations had been realized, and that we had already been amply repaid for the difficulties, privations and dangers, that we had encountered in our toilsome journey towards this fairyland of sport.'

Harris spent three weeks in the grasslands and forests of the western Transvaal, shot several elephants and lost many more. Then he turned southwards and arrived back in the Colony at the end of January 1837.

It had been an expensive expedition. Harris estimated the cost at £800, but besides the financial outlay his expedition had lost seventy oxen and a number of horses. On the credit side the young pioneer brought back with him complete heads of every species of game animal, a variety of skins, a folio of detailed wild life drawings and a quantity of elephant and hippopotamus ivory. From his experiences, Harris had this advice for other would-be African adventurers:

'. . . by entertaining a sufficient number of Europeans to keep the Hottentots in awe; and employing also a third waggon to carry out grain for the best horses, as well as to bring back ivory and more quadrupeds to the Colony, the expedition might be made to cover its own expenses.'

This became the pattern for most subsequent expeditions. The sportsmen planned to enjoy some first-class unrestricted shooting and to collect enough ivory to pay all the costs of the trip. Half a century later the same ideas were prevalent when Frederick Jackson and his friend Rider Haggard were contemplating a safari:

'. . . it was suggested that Rider, his wife, and I should go out there for a year, and have the time of our lives. Between us, he and I were to pay all expenses from the proceeds of elephant-hunting; and during the intervals between such trips, he was to write his books, while I was to amuse myself with smaller game, including all the known South African antelopes, as well as the local East African ones, such as topi, lesser kudu, etc., etc., birds and butterflies. It was altogether most alluring.'

The first man to be stirred to emulation of Harris' exploits was Roualeyn George Gordon Cumming, who shot elephants over much the same ground as Harris between 1843 and 1848. One way and another Cumming made an appreciable sum of money out of hunting in Africa. He amassed a considerable amount of ivory and a large personal museum of game trophies. On his return to England he wrote a self-congratulatory account of his exploits—*Five Year's of a Hunter's Life in the Far Interior of South Africa* (later a shorter and even more highly coloured, popular version, modestly entitled *The Lion Hunter of South Africa*, was published). This was the first commercial book written about big game hunting in Africa and it was an instant success. Cumming became the darling of London society. In 1851 his trophies were put on display at the Great Exhibition to the general amazement of the populace. Cumming toured the country giving lectures and later showed his exhibits in a prominent site where, for a modest fee, the public could gaze at lions, giraffe, buffalo and elephants, wondering at the bravery of the man who had shot these fierce creatures.

That the young Scot was brave there can be no doubt. About his skill as a hunter, his truthfulness as a raconteur and his general probity in dealing with the people and animals of Africa it is not so easy to be confident. If we are to believe his word almost every man he encountered of whatever race was a scoundrel, a fool or a coward—many were, apparently, all three. The trader whose advice he took on equipping his expedition was only of value to Cumming 'during his sober interludes'. His head-servant, a cockney called Long, was 'inclined more to worship at the shrine of Venus than at that of Diana'. His Khoikhoi servants were, to a man, sulky, boastful and cowardly, frequently needing 'a little wholesome correction with the jambok'. Whenever Cumming missed bringing down a fine specimen it was almost always, apparently, the fault of one or other of his attendants.

The young Scottish laird did not want for capital and was able to set off from the Colony with three waggons, stuffed with enough provisions and trade goods to stock a Highland grocer, ironmonger and milliner for a whole year, a hundred draught oxen, tents, horses and hunting dogs. Cumming was determined to obtain his trophies by whatever means presented themselves. Trade played an important part in his expedition. Unlike more circumspect travellers he was prepared to give the Africans what they most desired in exchange for ivory—i.e. guns—and so he loaded up many cases of old muskets in Grahamstown. These stood him in good stead when he reached Bamangwato territory, although bargaining with Chief Sekhomi took up five days:

'Although I voted the trading an intense bore, it was nevertheless well worth a little time and inconvenience, on account of the enormous profit I should realise. The price I had paid for the muskets was £16 for each case containing twenty muskets; and the value of the ivory I required for each musket was upwards of £30, being about 3,000 percent., which I am informed is reckoned among mercantile men to be a very fair profit.'

Sekhomi's territory lay in the land between the Kalahari desert and the upper Limpopo and his capital, Shoshong, became an important stopping place for the increasing numbers of hunters, missionaries, prospectors, adventurers and (later) colonizers making their way up into Central Africa. Sekhomi and his successors did very well out of trade with the white man. The chief had a large and perpetually replenished stock of ivory. It was obtained by his own hunters and from Sekhomi's San vassals, from whom it was extracted as tribute. With guns they obtained from trade, the Bamangwato were able to hold their own against the Ndebele and other wandering victims of the Mfecane.

It was in Bamangwato territory that Cumming found the elephant herds he had been seeking. Like Harris and others he was filled with great excitement at the prospect of shooting his first tusker. Deliberately ingoring a group of five bulls, Cumming singled out for destruction a female accompanied by her calf:

'. . . I let fly at her head a little behind the eye. She got it hard and sharp, just where I aimed, but it did not seem to affect her much. Uttering a loud cry, she wheeled about, when I gave her the second ball, close behind the shoulder. All the elephants uttered a strange rumbling noise, and made off in a line to northward at a brisk ambling pace. . . . I did not wait to load, but ran back to the hillock to obtain a view . . . they were standing in a grove of shady trees, but the wounded one was some distance behind with another elephant, doubtless its particular friend, who was endeavouring to assist it. . . . Presently my men hove in sight, bringing the dogs; and when these came up I waited some time before commencing the attack, that the dogs and horses might recover their wind. We then rode slowly towards the elephants . . . the wounded one immediately dropped astern, and next moment she was surrounded by the dogs, which, barking angrily, seemed to engross her attention.

'Having placed myself between her and the retreating troop I dismounted to fire within forty yards of her, in open ground. Colesberg (Cumming's horse) was extremely afraid of the elephants, and gave me much trouble, jerking my arm when I tried to fire. At length I let fly; but on endeavouring to regain my saddle, Colesberg declined to allow me to mount; and when I tried to lead him, and run for it, he only backed towards the wounded elephant. At this moment I heard another elephant close behind; and on looking about I beheld the "friend", with uplifted trunk, charging down upon me at top speed, shrilly trumpeting and following an old black pointer named Schwart, that was perfectly deaf, and trotted along before the enraged elephant quite unaware of what was behind him. I felt certain she would have either me or my horse. I however decided not to relinquish my steed, but to hold on by the bridle. My men, who of course kept at a safe distance, stood aghast with their mouths open, and for a few seconds my position was certainly not an enviable one. Fortunately, however, the dogs took off the attention of the elephant; and just as they were upon me I managed to spring into the saddle, where I was safe. As I turned my back to mount, the elephants were so very near that I really expected to feel one of their trunks lay hold of me. I rode up to Klein-boy, for my double-barrelled two-grooved rifle; he and Isaac were pale and almost speechless with fright. Returning to the charge, I was soon once more alongside, and, firing from the saddle, I sent another brace of bullets into the wounded elephant. Colesberg was extremely unsteady, and destroyed the correctness of my aim.

'The friend now seemed resolved to do some mischief, and charged me furiously, pursuing me to a distance of several hundred yards. I therefore deemed it proper to give her a gentle hint to act less officiously, and accordingly, having loaded, I approached within thirty yards, and gave her a sharp, right and left, behind the shoulder, upon which she at once made off with a drooping trunk, evidently with a mortal wound. . . . I foolishly allowed her to escape, while I amused myself with the first, which kept walking backwards and standing by every tree she passed. Two more shots finished her: on receiving them she tossed her trunk up and down two or three times, and, falling on her broadside against a thorny tree, which yielded like grass before her enormous weight, she uttered a deep hoarse cry and expired.'

Cumming included an illustration of this incident in *Five Years of a Hunter's Life* which shows an enraged cow elephant with vicious tusks bearing down furiously upon the distracted hunter and about two paces from him. Presumably such displays of artistic licence inspired our Victorian forbears, dependent as they were on books such as Cumming's for their knowledge of the 'Dark Continent'.

Subsequently Cumming never deliberately came into close quarters with elephant, preferring to shoot from a range of sixty or seventy yards. Hunting from horseback was a very skilled occupation, particularly with muzzle-loading guns such as were used until the second half of the century. Incredible as it may seem Cumming and contemporary sportsmen could re-load these cumbersome weapons with powder and shot while galloping over rough country, keeping one eye on the gun, another on their quarry and, apparently, a third on the terrain immediately ahead. They were truly magnificent handlers of horse and gun.

Shooting from horseback gave the elephant hunters much greater mobility, but it also presented them with problems. On the one hand they could pursue panicking herds, separate a fine tusker from his companions or follow a trail for hours through thick bush. On the other they might have to leave their waggons and supplies for many hours or days. Cumming always made sure he was 'tolerably comfortable' when away from his base. He parcelled up the following essentials which were carried by locally hired porters: blanket, change of clothing, nightcap, ammunition, coffee, bread, sugar, pepper, salt, meat, bowl, teaspoon, kettle, water, axes and sickles.

Cumming made five journeys to the prime hunting grounds in Bamangwato country and shot over a hundred elephants. Then he decided that 'in the most laborious pursuit of elephant-hunting I was overtaxing my frame' and returned to England to turn his tales and trophies into hard cash. At Colesberg Cumming met another young hunter who was setting out for the interior and was able to give the newcomer the benefit of his advice as well as sell him some oxen.

The newcomer was one of the most famous sportsmen ever to venture into the 'Dark Continent' and was destined to win himself the nickname of 'the Nimrod of South Africa'. William Cotton Oswell certainly looked the part—tall, slim, keen-eyed and handsome, he was an excellent horseman and a fine shot. In his attitude to South African sport he was a complete contrast to Cumming. He was not interested in trade and claimed in later life that if any African had tried to barter ivory for guns he would have struck the fellow down. He always made a point of getting in as close as possible to a quarry in order to despatch it with the least possible suffering. Cumming records one occasion on which he incapacitated a bull elephant and 'resolved to devote a short time to the contemplation of this noble elephant before I should lay him low'. He lit a fire a few yards from the immobile beast, brewed and drank a calm cup of coffee, then decided on an interesting experiment to discover where elephants are most vulnerable to fatal shots. 'I fired several bullets at different parts of the enormous skull.' After this it still took the kilted hero of the veldt a dozen shots to kill the unfortunate animal. Cotton Oswell had that true sportsman's love of the animals he pursued which a non-hunter finds impossible to understand. On many occasions he was so impressed by the beauty, grandeur or courage of an animal that he resisted his hunter's instinct to go in for the kill. And of the human animals who journeyed with him he said 'I had the best of companions . . . and capital servants, who stuck to me throughout. I never had occasion to raise a hand against a native.' Despite the entreaties of friends and fellow sportsmen he could never be prevailed upon to write his memoirs. Only in old age did he contribute a couple of chapters to a hunting anthology. Yet he became a legend in his own lifetime and has remained so in sporting circles ever since.

William Cotton Oswell travelled widely through the unexplored regions of southern Africa between 1844 and 1853. He accompanied Livingstone on the expeditions which discovered Lake Ngami and reached the Zambezi. It might be said that Oswell made those expeditions possible for he contributed considerably to their cost and kept Livingstone's entourage provided with fresh meat. Livingstone thought highly of Oswell, indeed Oswell was one of the very few European companions Livingstone could tolerate.

Though Oswell shot every kind of South African game animal there is no doubt where his preference lay:

'There have been discussions as to who is king among the beasts, and to this day the lion is generally given the title. But look down that narrow game-track. A lion is coming up it from the water. As he turns the curve in the winding path he sees that a rhinoceros or buffalo is coming down to drink. He slinks onto the bush, lies very low, gives them the road, lets them pass well by, and then resumes his interrupted way. If this is the King, he is exceedingly courteous to his subjects —one might even think just a little in awe of some of them. King of the cats in Africa he may be, and is; but king of the beasts he is not.

'Come with me to a desert pool some clear moonlight night

when the shadows are deep and sharply cut, and the moon
herself, in the dry, cloudless air, looks like a ball. All is nearly
as bright as day, only the light is silver, not gold. Sit down
on that rock and watch the thirsty anim alsas they drink—
buffalo, rhinoceros, antelope, quagga, and occasionally, if the
water is large, lions too. But what has frightened the antelope
and the quagga that they throw their heads up for a second
and fade away into the shadows? The other beasts too are
listening, and now leave the sides of the pond. Nothing but
the inevitable, irrepressible jackal, that *gamin* amongst wild
things, remains in view. As yet your dull human ears have
caught no sound, but very soon the heavy tread, and low,
rumbling note of an oncoming herd of elephants reaches you.
They are at the water. The jackals have sat down with their
tails straight out behind them, but not another creature is to
be seen. The King drinks. . . . He squirts the water over his
back, makes the whole pool muddy, and retires solemnly,
leaving his subjects, who now gather round to make the best
of what he has fouled. This is the King in the opinion of the
beasts.'

What a pity that William Cotton Oswell's modesty has deprived
sporting literature of many more such passages.

When the Nimrod of South Africa set out onto the veldt he
could be almost blasé about the abundance of animals. There
was never any worry about finding enough meat for the pot.
With one gun, he estimated that a hunter could feed eight
hundred men for several months. Oswell and his companions
thought nothing of shooting eland for their fat when they
needed more candles. On many occasions his gun was wielded
not for the sake of gaining trophies or even of feeding his own
men, but providing meat for the local people. Because of his
reputation as an elephant hunter Oswell never lacked for
hunters and guides who were hired to him by their chiefs in
return for elephant meat.

The skill and care which Oswell cultivated in order to kill
copiously but cleanly is shown in his own description of his
technique:

'Most of my elephants were killed from horseback with the

shoulder-shot; the cover is rarely thick enough to allow you to get within reach on foot. Besides, on foot you can seldom dispose of more than two at a time; whereas from horseback, under favourable conditions, you may double or even treble that number. Sometimes you must crawl in, and then, of course, you take the head shot if you can get it; but you ought to be within fifteen yards, on a line parallel with your quarry, just a trifle in advance, and then a ball in the lower depression, or temple, will, nineteen times out of twenty, be instantly fatal. . . . In tolerable ground there is but little difficulty; but in thick bush there is always some danger, more especially if you are particular in choosing your tusks; and in riding the bull you select out of the herd there is a certain amount of knack—you settle to him and then press him individually, disregarding the rest of the herd for the time. He shoots ahead of his companions or turns round on you and charges; in either case you have gained your object— separation. If he charges, put the horse to the gallop and let him follow you, the further the better. Watch as he slacks off, keeping about twenty yards ahead, and pull up sharp when he comes to a stand. He is too blown to charge again, and when he turns to go after his mates he must give you his side; one or two shots properly placed at short range are enough, and you are away again after the flying herd. The oftener you attack the easier the victory, for the heavy beasts get tired, and in consequence are much less difficult to kill.'

To choose to stalk these enormous beasts at close quarters denotes courage, but deliberately to provoke them to chase you across uneven ground is bravery of a high order. For all his size the elephant is capable of considerable speed in short bursts so that the result of a race between horse and elephant over rough country is by no means a foregone conclusion. M. Daly, who hunted throughout most of East Africa in the early years of the twentieth century, describes how he timed a charging elephant in the Kenya Highlands:

'The chance came one afternoon in the bush through which the elephants had made quite an avenue, starting from a cool forest stream and ending between two large boulders some twenty feet high from the ground. Here, having drunk at the stream, turned round, and about to start leisurely up the avenue, stood a great young bull, and we . . . seized the opportunity to hurry it on its way and time it.

'Timer ready, bang! went the shot and off went the elephant, and, like a great ball of smoke, shot through the archway and disappeared.

'The time was exactly ten seconds: the carefully measured distance was a hundred and twenty yards. . . .'

It is not surprising that Oswell had many close shaves during his elephant-hunting career. The worst occurred while he was pursuing a wounded tusker through very dense bush. Bending low over the horse's neck to avoid low branches, his legs and arms torn by savage thorns, Oswell was startled to see his prey suddenly turn round and charge. With difficulty the hunter turned his steed:

'Battered and torn by branch and thorn I managed a kind of gallop, but it was impossible to keep it up. The elephant thundered straight through obstacles we were obliged to go round, and in fifty yards we were fast in a thick bush and he within fifteen of us. As a last chance I tried to get off, but in rolling round on my saddle my spur gored the pony's flank, and the elephant screaming over him at the same moment, he made a convulsive effort and freed himself, depositing me in a sitting position immediately in front of the uplifted forefoot of the charging bull. So near was it that I mechanically opened my knees to allow him to put it down and, throwing myself back, crossed my hands upon my chest, obstinately puffing myself out with the idea of trying to resist the gigantic tread, or at all events of being as troublesome to crush as possible. I saw the burly brute from chest to tail as he passed directly over me lengthways, one foot between my knees, and one fourteen inches beyond my head, and not a graze! Five tons at least! . . . One hears of nightmares—well, for a month or more I dare say, I had nightelephants.'

The gun that William Cotton Oswell used throughout his adventures became a famous hunting relic in its own right. It was a No. 10 calibre muzzle-loading Purdy made specially for him. It fired a spherical ball and each shot required three-quarters of an ounce of powder. In 1861, when Oswell's hunting days were over, he lent the gun to Samuel Baker who used it on his famous journey in search of the Nile. Baker records that the weapon, though firing true, was already badly scratched and battered as a result of its owner's frequent headlong pursuit of game through thick bush. The gun was dutifully returned to its owner but minus the ramrod, an omission which as Baker explained resulted from an incident in the Sudan:

'My man (a native) was attacked, and being mobbed during the act of loading, he was obliged to fire at the most prominent assailant before he had time to withdraw his ramrod. This passed through the attacker's body, and was gone beyond hope of recovery.'

William Charles Baldwin hunted throughout south-eastern and central Africa between 1852 and 1860. He first encountered elephant in nothern Zululand but had to trek across the Transvaal and 150 miles beyond the Limpopo before he found any sizeable herds. Eventually his search assumed the character of a pilgrimage. Following local reports of large herds just ahead, he travelled on and on until he reached the mighty Zambezi just below Victoria Falls, over 1,200 miles from his starting point at Durban. He limped back in to the Colony tattered, drawn and alone having endured long months crossing waterless country, barren of wild life, having buried four white companions, watched his horses and dogs die, lost most of his oxen and been deserted by all but a few of his men. He had set out full of youthful enthusiasm, but after eight years of expeditions his *joie de vivre* had evaporated and the later entries in his journal show him to have been sated with hunting:

'I have bagged this time with great difficulty one pallah and one springbuck, and should be very glad if I had with me any young sportsman to take this job off my hands, as it begins now to pall upon me, and, as soon as ever I have procured sufficient for the day, I immediately make the best of my way back. It is no longer sport; the days are now gone by when I would walk from Leyland or Highton to Brinseall and back, for the chance only of a shot or two at a snipe . . .'

But *Loxodonta africana* provided Baldwin with many thrills and a goodly number of valuable tusks during those eight years. Hunters disagree about which game animal is the most dangerous. Lion, leopard, buffalo and rhino all have their champions. Some have regarded the elephant as a big bluffer and certainly he often uses the tactics of intimidation to ward off an enemy. He will charge forward trumpeting ferociously, waving his trunk, flapping his ears, only to stop at a few yards distance. But any hunter who has seriously devoted his attention to elephants has learned to take nothing for granted when confronted by an angry or wounded tusker. Baldwin on at least one occasion had ample proof of elephant tenacity.

He was hunting on foot in thick bush and had wounded an old bull, which immediately turned on him. Baldwin ran up a nearby hillside trusting to his supposed agility on sloping ground. But the vegetation was wet with recent rain and the hunter slipped and slithered upwards at a very poor speed. The enraged elephant had no difficulty in gaining on him. Baldwin decided to change tactics. Stopping abruptly he turned to the right and set off down the flank of the hill. Surely the lumbering beast would be wary of charging downhill. Not so; the monster turned and followed its quarry, 'screaming and trumpeting in full career after me at a tremendous pace. He must have been over me in a few strides more, when I sprang to the right, and down he went in his mad career, crashing and carrying all before him, utterly unable to stop if he had wished, as the hill was very steep, and he was under full sail.' Baldwin resolved after this incident always to hunt from horseback.

As he drew closer to the Zambezi, Baldwin entered country where two new problems faced the ivory hunter. These problems were established commerce and tsetse fly. The Zambezi valley was part of a network of trade routes, which covered Central Africa. For generations long distance traders had conveyed along these tracks ivory and slaves destined for the export centres of Sofala, Qualimane, Mozambique, Benguela and

Luanda. Understandably the local people were not anxious to assist the white ivory hunter who suddenly appeared in their midst. Baldwin found he could no longer count on being guided to waterholes, sold food or told where the elephant herds were. Entries like this became common in his journal:

'July 22nd [1859] . . . It is now the depth of winter, and the grass is as dry as old tinder, without the slightest nourishment in it. As a natural consequence, the oxen are as lean as rakes, and, worst of all, the mealies and Kaffir corn are finished, and no more is to be had at any price, so that we cannot long hold out under these circumstances. I grieve much for the poor willing horses, thirteen or fourteen hours under the saddle, at foot's pace, in a broiling sun three-fourths of the time, then tied up to the waggon without food, and stinted in their allowance of water, which we have to draw ten miles, at least, half the way through hack-thorns over stony ground. These are among the hardships we must undergo to get elephants; they are dearly paid for . . .'

No wonder that Baldwin concluded 'Elephant hunting is the very hardest life a man can chalk out for himself'.

The tsetse fly was prevalent everywhere north of the Zambesi and in many areas south of it. In the mid-nineteeth century this little *Tabanidae* was death to all domestic animals. Baldwin went in constant fear of wandering inadvertently into 'fly-country' and did, in fact, lose some of his oxen from tsetse bites. Yet the fortunes of an otherwise not over-successful expedition were restored by some of his followers who got lost and did wander into fly-country. Boccas, his head-man set off with one wagon when Baldwin was camped near the Chobe River, a tributary of the Zambezi. The trusted Khoikhoi, who was a superb shot, failed to turn up at the rendezvous and after waiting several days, Baldwin had to give his wagon up for lost. But when he had been six weeks at Durban the triumphant Boccas suddenly burst into town driving a wagon overflowing with tusks. In the inhospitable tsetse country he had come across large herds of elephant and with no competition had had a field day. So much ivory did he collect that he had to throw out of the wagon all Baldwin's skins and trophies to make room for it. Boccas was only one of a new breed of African hunters who mastered new methods of hunting while in the pay of European sportsmen.

Let us allow William Cotton Oswell the last word. This greatest of all pioneer hunters had this to say when, towards the end of his life he reminisced about the early days in Africa:

'There is a fascination to me in the remembrance of the past in all its connections: the free life, the self-dependence, the boring into what was then a new country; the feeling as you lay under your canvas that you were looking at the stars from a point on the earth whence no other European had ever seen them; the hope that every patch of bush, every little rise, was the only thing between you and some strange sight or scene—these are with me still; and were I not a married man with children and grandchildren, I believe I should head back into Africa again, and end my days in the open air. It is useless to tell me of the advantages of civilisa-tion; civilised man runs wild much easier and sooner than the savage becomes tame . . . Take the word of one who has tried both states: there are charms in the wild; the ever-increasing, never satisfied needs of the tame my soul cannot away with.

'But I am writing of close upon fifty years ago. Africa is nearly used up; she belongs no more to the Africans and the beasts; Boers, gold-seekers, diamond-miners and experi-mental farmers—all of them (from my point of view) mistakes—have changed the face of her. A man must be a first-rate sportsman now to keep himself and his family; houses stand where we once shot elephants, and the railway train will soon be whistling and screaming through all hunting-fields south of the Zambesi.'

4

'Ivory! always ivory! What a curse the elephant has been to Africans!'

—A. J. Swann, FIGHTING THE SLAVE-HUNTERS
IN CENTRAL AFRICA

Trader Extraordinary

While the white hunters were slowly moving up from the Cape
the vast interior of Central Africa lay largely in the grip of the
Arab slavers and their allies. In the bush where success made
its own laws some of these ruthless traders had made themselves
into kings. They ruled purely for reasons of personal gain and
did not bother to give excuses for their dominion. It was left to
their European successors to lay claim to a civilising mission
and to talk about the white man's burden. The Arabs were at
least honest: they were there to amass ivory. It was in pursuit
of wealth that they gained dominion over men and territory,
ruled kingdoms and overswayed kings. They were not ashamed
to admit that their empires were built on the bones of African
men and African elephants.

Of all these 'emperors' the best known and the greatest—if
we strip that word of all moral connotations—was Tippu Tip.
Tippu Tip, 'the Blinker', was the son of one of the leading Arab
merchants by a Zanzibar lady of mixed descent. Though there
was, presumably, more Arab blood in him than in many of his
contemporaries who called themselves Arabs, his features were
conspicuously negroid. He was ugly in a squash-faced way and
he suffered from a tremulous, nervous twitching of the eyelids
which gave him his nickname, Tippu Tip. It need not be
thought that this epithet was applied in mockery; Tippu Tip's
twitch was most noticeable at times of emotional stress and
many a man had cause to quake when the lids began to flicker
over Tippu's angry eyes.

Tippu Tip's full patronymic was Hamed bin Muhammad el
Murjebi. His grandfather, Juba bin Rajab was among the first

Zanzibaris to tread the Bagamoyo-Ujiji caravan route. He took pains to cultivate the friendship of the Nyamwezi Chief of the Tabora district, Fundikira, and even arranged a childhood marriage between his own son, Muhammad, and Karunde, one of the chief's daughters. It is not surprising, therefore, that Muhammad, when he began trading on his own account, used this area as his base. With Fundikira's support, he became both prosperous and well-respected. When Tippu Tip spoke in later years about his father he could not refrain from typical Arab exaggeration, yet even from this biased account we can see something of the prestige Muhammad bin Rajab el Murjebi enjoyed:

'. . . my father was greatly respected. Whatever he wanted in and around Tabora he got, and when he went down to the coast he took his wife Karunde. He was also given other goods, was my father, and at this time he was as though Chief in the Nyamwezi manner, having much property and many followers, perhaps even as much as the Chiefs of Uganda and Karagwe.'

Muhammad was the acknowledged leader of the merchant community of Tabora, the Arab suburb which grew up beside Fundikira's capital of Uyanyembe*, and he spent most of his time either there or on trading expeditions in the interior. Hamed, meanwhile, was brought up by his mother's people in Zanzibar. It was not until he was eighteen that his father took him on an inland trading voyage that led him to Lake Tanganyika and beyond. The youth learned rapidly the methods that were necessary for commercial success in the interior, and soon showed those characteristics of shrewdness, vigour, determination and ruthlessness which were to make him the greatest of all the Zanzibaris.

The lad showed his spirit on this very first expedition. When the caravan reached Ujiji his father had to turn back on receiving disturbing news from Unyanyembe. Fundikira lay

---

* Unyanyembe is modern Tabora. The Arab settlement alongside the old Nyamwezi capital was known as Tabora. As the Arab town gradually engulfed the African village the name 'Tabora' came to be used for the whole place.

dying and a political crisis was brewing over the succession. Muhammad decided to leave the expedition in the hands of an experienced kinsman, who would lead it into the little known land of Urua,* beyond the lake. Tippu Tip was outraged. 'I can't go on to Urua, with our property in the possession of a man from the Mrima coast, and I following along with him. Better that I return with you.' After some argument Muhammad reluctantly allowed Tippu Tip to take charge of the caravan. So the young man gained his first sight of the land he was later to dominate.

Fundikira's death towards the end of 1858 led to the first serious breach of Afro-Arab relations. The new ruler, Mnwa Sele, had not been installed long before he began to grow alarmed at the growing power of the Zanzibaris and their control of the commercial life of his country. Seeing no reason why the foreigners should be the major beneficiaries from trade in his territory he reversed Fundikira's policy by imposing a customs duty—*hongo*—on caravans passing through the capital. This, the Tabora community grudgingly accepted. But when Mnwa Sele went on to make other unwelcome demonstrations of his authority† the Arabs decided that their host had become too powerful. Led by Muhammad bin Juma they combined to drive the chief out of his capital. Tippu Tip, returning from the Urua safari, was just in time to take part in this coup.

Mnwa Sele's overthrow was all too easy for the Zanzibaris. Not only were they better equipped with guns and powder; they were confronting a society which was breaking up as a result of internal and external pressures. From the south-west wild bands of invaders, called Ngoni, were spreading over the

---

* Frequently in African languages a prefix is used to denote 'land of'. Thus 'Urua' is 'the land of the Rua'. Other similar place names used in this chapter are Utetela and Itabwa.

† The last straw as far as Tippu Tip's father was concerned was the execution of his mother-in-law (Karunde's mother). Mnwa Sele considered the old woman to be implicated in a palace intrigue and meted out, according to custom, summary justice. But Muhammad regarded this as an insult and an attack upon his own family circle.

land. The nucleus of these warlike groups were immigrants from distant south-east Africa who had been driven out earlier in the century by the Zulu expansion begun by Shaka. By the 1850s, the Ngoni were a vast, restless, heterogeneous band of marauders, who had, seemingly, forsaken any search for new land, preferring instead a life of brigandage, plunder and rapine. Their warrior bands, known as *ruga-ruga*, struck terror into the hearts of all who confronted them. They wore cloth stained with the blood of their victims, caps made of human skulls, belts of entrails and necklaces of teeth. They were united only by the iron discipline imposed by their warlords and by their lust for blood and plunder.

Chiefs left their chiefdoms to organise safaris, thus easing the task of rivals and ambitious neighbours. Young men hired themselves out as ivory porters for months and years at a time and were thus not around to defend their homeland at times of crisis. The ivory trade introduced a new economy based on fierce capitalist competition. It enriched commoners and enabled them to challenge the hereditary authority of their chiefs. It brought large numbers of guns into eastern and central Africa. It encouraged African leaders to invade the territory of their neighbours in search of elephants and slaves. It challenged the leaders of society to decide whether they were going to stand by the old traditions or try to adapt to the bewildering new dynamics.

These external pressures aggravated existing divisions and rivalries within African society. When the Tabora Arabs deposed Mnwa Sele they did so with the support of a relative, Mkasiwa, who coveted the chieftaincy. Mkasiwa was duly placed on the throne but he was little more than a puppet chief. Other Nyamwezi princes refused to accept the political change and flocked to the camp of Mnwa Sele who continued to attack enemies and raid caravans until his death in 1865. Then other champions emerged to lead the anti-Arab crusade. These African leaders organised their own war bands along the lines of the *ruga-ruga*. By terrorism and intrigue they enlarged their inherited chieftaincies into considerable empires. They also wrought havoc along the caravan routes.

Because of the disturbed state of central Tanzania Tippu Tip decided to seek his fortune elsewhere. Soon after the trouble at

Tabora, he was ready to start organising his own trading ventures. Having obtained backers he made a number of journeys in the 1860s always taking the routes towards the northern end of Lake Nyasa, which skirted the more troubled areas. He usually hired porters at the coast or from the country he passed through. Strong, able-bodied men who were prepared to commit themselves to a long safari were preferable to unwilling slaves who had to be guarded carefully and whose chains slowed down the caravan.

But porters could be troublesome and dishonest. Tippu Tip found this on the early stages of the journey he began in 1866. He hired 700 Zaramo porters at the coast. The Zaramo usually disdained this kind of labour but a recent famine had made food so scarce and expensive that the young men were reluctantly persuaded to sell their services to Tippu Tip, since this was the only way they could be sure of filling their stomachs. The first stage of the journey took them sixty miles to Mkamba. There Tippu Tip called a halt and issued six days' rations to the men, for ahead of them lay several days' march through barren land towards the Rufiji river. To give unwilling workers a plentiful supply of food was a tactical error, as the Arabs soon discovered:

'On the day we decided to leave, the porters were scattered throughout the many villages where they had set down their loads, a hundred men in one, sixty in another; they had dispersed.

'In the morning we sounded the departure drum. There was no response. We sent out men to go and hurry them up but they encountered no one. All had deserted. When they brought me this news, I went myself to look in the villages where they had set down their loads. I saw no one. I lost my temper and brought the news to my brother and told him to bring me my guns, travelling clothes and a bed-roll and servants. Then I went back through the districts of Mbezi and Ndengereko. Within a few hours I had a force of eighty guns. I slept on the road and on the second day arrived in the porters' villages, but they had not yet arrived. I seized their elders and kinsmen, about 200 of them, and bound them up. Thereupon they beat their drums and met together, the whole lot of them. When they saw that we were ready they came back. I went on ahead to Ndengereko and then to Mbezi, seizing a large number of people. I went into every part of Zaramu country and in the space of five days had seized 800 men. They called me Kingugwa Chui* because the leopard attacks indiscriminately, here and there. I yoked the whole lot of them together and went back with them to Mkamba.

'From there I went on to Zerere in the country behind Kwale, where a Banyan was living, by name Hila . . . I asked him for strips of metal, and he gave me as much as I wanted. These I took back to Mkamba and the craftsmen who were with me made chains. I put the whole lot of the porters in these chains and sent my brother to go ahead of them while I followed behind, so that I could seize anyone who tried to escape. These locals called my brother Kumba-kumba, meaning he who has taken everyone.'

Tippu Tip's matter of fact account, which does not even trouble to be boastful, indicates how narrow was the line dividing paid labour from slave labour in Africa. Professional porters were preferred but where they were unobtainable or where extra workers were needed, the caravan leaders would resort to captive porterage.

Tippu Tip's caravan reached the Rufiji and turned westwards up-river. For weeks they marched in search of elephants or African leaders from whom they could buy ivory. But the highlands north of Lake Nyasa had been well hunted for years and there was little ivory to be found. So the caravan moved on into the country of the Tabwa, south of Lake Tanganyika. The Tabwa were known to be rich in ivory, particularly the greatest of their chiefs, the elderly Nsama. Nsama also had another reputation—a reputation for greed and treachery. He disliked foreign traders, and those who passed through his territory did so at the risk of being plundered or killed. Tippu Tip's porters were terrified at the prospect of entering Itabwa and but for their chains they would probably have run away.

Tippu Tip marched straight to Nsama's capital to pay his respects and to present gifts of cloth and guns to the chief.

---

* 'The leopard who attacks without warning'.

Nsama received the Arabs courteously enough and showed them his enormous stocks of ivory. The chief's officers unlocked a number of large huts all stacked to the roof with tusks. But this was mere braggadocio and not a prelude to trade, for the next day Nsama sent men to ambush his guests, with a view to capturing all their trade goods. But Tippu Tip turned the tables on his host. The Tabwa were driven back by superior musket fire and Tippu Tip's men went on to attack and capture the town.

Now, at one blow, Tippu Tip found himself the possessor of Nsama's most incredible horde of ivory. If his word is to be believed the total cache weighed 1,950 frasila (about 30 tons). Nsama's warehouses also yielded up 700 frasila of copper and a large quantity of salt. In all, this one haul cannot have been worth less than £20,000 at current prices. A lucky strike indeed for a man leading his first long-distance caravan to the far interior. Tippu Tip made immediate plans to return to the coast. The first problem was transport. His ivory tusks—of which there must have been over 1,500—demanded many more men than he had with him, and in addition there was the copper, salt and all the expedition's unused loads of trade goods. It was time for the 'Leopard' to show his claws again. From Nsama's capital he immediately sent out a large raiding party, which came back with a thousand Tabwa slaves and over two thousand goats. Thus staffed and provisioned the expedition was ready to move on. Despite the large additional labour force the caravan could only proceed by three-hour relays. At the end of each march the porters had to be sent back to the previous stopping-place to pick up the remainder of the loads.

A few days later, on 29th July 1867, there occurred the brief meeting of two of the most remarkable travellers ever to enter Africa. David Livingstone had set out up the Rovuma river on what was to be his last journey early in 1866. Travelling slowly round Lake Nyasa and then crossing what is now northern Zambia he found himself in the vicinity of Tippu Tip's caravan and the whole countryside alive with the story of the Arab's recent conflict with Nsama. Livingstone was by this time in a bad way. He had lost all his medicines when two of his Yao porters had deserted six months before. Since then he had squelched through mosquito-infested swamps during the rainy

season and was now suffering the effects of hunger and fever.
Tippu Tip met up with the explorer at Ponda, near Lake Mweru.

For several days the Muslim slave trader was host to the
great Christian anti-slave trade crusader. And a good host he
made, too. According to Livingstone, Tippu Tip welcomed him
hospitably and courteously. He provided food for the missionary
and his men, freely gave any information he could about the
land and peoples and professed himself willing to be of any
material assistance he could to the white man. At Livingstone's
request he provided guides to take the explorer to various
places he wished to see. He promised to see that certain of
Livingstone's boxes were safely sent up from the coast to Ujiji.
He finally despatched more guides to go with Livingstone to the
great King Kazembe and gave the missionary letters of introduction. Tippu Tip put himself to considerable trouble to help
Livingstone and certainly delayed his own departure for the
coast. This was typical of his attitude towards the white men
he occasionally met in the interior. It was something he took a
pride in; something that touched his honour. He even boasted
about it later to A. J. Swann:

'Who helped Cameron, Speke, Livingstone? . . . Who saved
your life, and those of all your party; was it not me? Have I
attempted to hinder any missionaries, although they are not
of my religion and hate my business of catching slaves? Tell
me! Is there a single European traveller who can honestly
say I was not his friend?'

There was much truth in the Arab's boast. Most of the
explorers and missionaries who passed through East and
Central Africa in the late nineteenth century had cause to be
grateful to Tippu Tip for assistance at some stage of their
journeyings. Even when it became obvious to the Arabs that
the white man was coming to force him out of his traditional
haunts, Tippu Tip and several of his colleagues continued to
give courteous assistance to individual Europeans.

After seeing Livingstone safely on his way, Tippu Tip
resumed his journey to the coast. Even after repaying the
banyans at their exorbitant rates of interest he must have had
enough money left to live very comfortably indeed at Zanzibar,

but it was not in the nature of the man to retire. In any case he was actively encouraged to return to the interior by no less a person than Sultan Majid of Zanzibar. Only a few years previously Majid had lost control of his ancestral homeland, Oman, when the Sultanate of Oman and Zanzibar had been divided between himself and his brother, Thuwain. Majid was now determined to extend his rule over the East African mainland, so obviously rich in ivory and slaves. He decided to move his capital to the coast opposite Zanzibar and, in 1866, work began on a new palace complex overlooking a wide sweep of coral sand that enclosed a large natural harbour. Locally this idyllic spot was known as Haven of Peace—*Dar es Salaam*.

Sultan Majid had no resources for armed conquest of the interior; the extension of his influence had to be by means of the Zanzibari merchants. They were encouraged to make themselves powerful in inland localities and to rule these under the Sultan's flag. Tippu Tip was already known over a large area of the southern hinterland. Sultan Majid urged him to return as one of his lieutenants. Tippu Tip needed no encouragement. He had heard stories of ivory-rich lands further west, towards the region of the forest and the pygmies. No Arab had yet ventured to these lands and the people, innocent of commerce, had no notion of the value of elephant tusks. It was said that they left them rotting in the ground or used them to make fences. Early in 1870 he was ready to leave.

This time Tippu Tip spent twelve years in the interior, his longest absence from the coast. He travelled up to Tabora, where he found his father and the Arabs still having trouble with the interminable rivalries within the local ruling family and also with *ruga-ruga* raiders. After a few months he made the long trek southwestwards to the land of the Tabwa. Chief Nsama, who had regained his ransacked capital, now had a greater respect for the Arabs. He offered Tippu Tip no trouble but neither did he offer the olive branch. He maintained an attitude of sullen aloofness, refusing either to see Tippu Tip or to provide any assistance to his men.

Travelling westwards the expedition reached the great Lunda kingdom of Kazembe, south of Lake Mweru. The Eastern Lunda had dominated the commercial and political life of the region for over a century and a half and were still widely feared. But like other ancient African states Kazembe was finding it difficult to adapt to the rapidly changing world of the late nineteenth century. Arab caravans were becoming more frequent. To the south and east newly-formed states were expanding. The borders of Kazembe were being eroded. Arab traders were supplying its enemies with guns. By 1870 it had largely lost its control of the trade routes to the east coast.

The reigning king, Kazembe Muonga, reacted with alarm and hostility when he heard that the conqueror of Nsama was advancing towards his borders. By this time Tippu Tip's expedition, swelled by porters from Tabora, had assumed the porportions of a small army. He had at his command 4,000 men and 200 guns. Muonga, rather foolishly, tried to frighten his visitors away with some futile sabre-rattling. As Tippu Tip's men crossed into Kazembe they were greeted by an ineffective fusilade of spears and grapeshot. By this ill-considered demonstration Muonga was signing his own death warrant. An enraged Tippu Tip joined forces with some of the Kazembe's vassals, hired additional men and guns from some of his kinsmen settled around the southern end of Lake Tanganyika, and began a full-scale invasion of the kingdom.

The Arabs attacked and burned defenceless villages. They carried off into slavery, as Tippu Tip relates, 'countless men'. They took large quantities of ivory, grain and livestock. In a month they had fought their way through to the capital, overthrown and killed Muonga, and made themselves masters of his country. Tippu Tip appointed a new ruler and exacted a promise of annual tribute in the form of ivory, before he departed, driving his slaves and his booty before him.

Now Tippu Tip's fame preceded him wherever he went. To all African rulers he was not just another Zanzibari trader but the vanquisher of the mighty Nsama and Muonga. Chiefs hastened to send tribute in ivory as Tippu Tip's caravan approached so that the mighty warrior would pass by and leave them in peace.

But Tippu Tip did not always rely on brute force, as is shown by the way he gained a kingdom for himself in Utetela. He had been wandering for a year or so to the west of Lake Tanganyika, but became increasingly dissatisfied with commercial prospects in the region. There were too many coastal traders there. The local leaders had become familiar with the requirements of the Zanzibaris and had raised the price of ivory. So Tippu Tip turned his gaze further westward to the unknown lands where, rumour had it, there were still vast herds of elephant to be found and also unsophisticated peoples who did not know the value of ivory.

Not without difficulty Tippu Tip forced his men westwards to the borders of Tetela country, in the very centre of Africa. Information picked up on the way told him that the most promising area for ivory was the kingdom of Kasongo Rushie. This Tetela chief was reputed to be an old and lonely man, who years before had lost all his close relatives when the Rua invaded his territory. The old man therefore had to approach his end with the knowledge that he had no heir to succeed him. Tippu Tip took careful note of all the details of this story and the names of its chief characters. How he turned this news to good account can be best be explained in his own words. When Kasongo Rushie sent representatives to greet the Arab and enquire his business Tippu Tip replied:

' ". . . Utetela is also my country, Kasongo is related to me on my grandmother's side." They asked how this could be so. I told them, "A very long time ago the chief of Urua, Rungu Kabare Kumambe, waged war in all parts of the country, and reached Utetela. He took captive two women, Kina Darumamba and Kitoto, and took them to Urua. It happened that my grandfather, Habib bin Bushir el Wardi, my mother's father, came to Urua, and saw the two women, and bought one; taking her as concubine. Then my mother was born. . . . This grandmother of mine, Darumamba, used to tell me that in her home country she was a member of the royal house; that there was much ivory and many people and that I should make an effort to go there, although it was distant. She said her brother was a powerful chief, by name Kasongo Rushie Mwana Mapunga, and that all the Tetela and Kusu were his people . . ." '

The caravan was allowed to proceed while the envoys returned excitedly to report to their master. As soon as Tippu Tip came within a short distance of the capital Kasongo Rushie hurried out to greet his 'kinsman':

'In the morning about 8 a.m., the Chief and his men came all together and he said, "This is your chief, Tippu Tip! I have no longer any stake in the chieftainship; bring to him all the tusks. Anyone wanting anything should not come to me; authority lies with him." '

Thus, without striking a single blow, did Tippu Tip become an African chief. He stayed in his kingdom for over three years. Recognition as a legitimate ruler meant much more than prestige, authority and a comfortable life. A steady flow of ivory poured into the capital as tribute from vassal chiefs. Tippu Tip records that in the first fortnight of his reign he received two hundred tusks in this way. Kingship also lent a semblance of respectability to his slave and ivory raids on neighbouring states. Any pretext could be used for waging war and when Tippu Tip went on campaign he had at his back not only his own men, but a host of Tetela warriors. Soon new buildings were springing up in the capital—storehouses for King Tippu Tip's ivory and *bomas* (enclosures) for his slaves.

It is impossible to make an estimate of the amount of ivory that now accumulated at Tippu Tip's depot. Almost every day tusks arrived—the product of raiding, trading or tribute. At the end of three years his horde must have dwarfed even Nsama's cache which the Arab had captured seven years before. Even when Tippu Tip left Utetela in 1874 the tusks continued to pile up in his warehouses, for he left a regent to rule the kingdom in his absence and, according to Tippu Tip, this man, Mwinyi Dodi, was even more feared than Tippu Tip himself.

In the middle of 1874 Hamed bin Muhammad decided to set out for Manyema country to the north-east and particularly for the Zanzibari settlements of Nyangwe and Kassongo on the Lualaba. He had some guns which needed repairing but beyond that he had a yearning to see some more of his own people, and particularly his kinsmen.

Manyemaland was now swarming with Arab and half-caste traders who were making bloody havoc wherever they went.

The leading coast men at this time were Mwinyi Dagumbi and Mtagamoyo. An incident witnessed by David Livingstone at Nyangwe in 1871 indicates the senseless barbarity these men encouraged (or, at least, failed to prevent) on the part of their followers:

'It was a hot, sultry day, and when I went into the market I saw Adie and Manilla, and three of the men who had lately come with Dagumbi. I was surprised to see these three with their guns, and felt inclined to reprove them . . . for bringing weapons into the market, but I attributed it to their ignorance, and, it being very hot, I was walking away to go out of the market, when I saw one of the fellows haggling about a fowl, and seizing hold of it. Before I had got thirty yards out, the discharge of two guns in the middle of the crowd told me that slaughter had begun: crowds dashed off from the place, and threw down their wares in confusion, and ran. At the same time . . . volleys were discharged from a party down near the creek on the panic-stricken women, who dashed at the canoes. These, some fifty or more, were jammed in the creek, and the men forgot their paddles in the terror that seized all. The canoes were not to be got out, for the creek was too small for so many; men and women, wounded by the balls, poured into them, and leaped and scrambled into the water, shrieking. A long line of heads in the river showed that great numbers struck out for an island a full mile off . . . if they had struck away diagonally to the opposite bank, the current would have aided them, and, though nearly three miles off, some would have gained land: as it was, the heads above water showed the long line of those that would inevitably perish.

'Shot after shot continued to be fired on the helpless and perishing. Some of the long line of heads disappeared quietly; whilst other poor creatures threw their arms high, as if appealing to the great Father above, and sank . . . the Arabs themselves estimated the loss of life at between 330 and 400 souls. The shooting-party near the canoes were so reckless, they killed two of their own people.'

There is no reason to believe that Livingstone was the unfortunate and unwilling witness of a unique tragedy. Life for the Zanzibaris in the interior was compounded of organised raids and warfare and feuds between rival groups of traders. Violence was their bedfellow. Contempt for the *Washenzi* (as they called the Africans) was second nature to them. Any commercial frustration, imagined insult or petty annoyance could lead to such an outbreak as the Manyema massacre. Yet it is interesting to note that most of the European observers who recorded and condemned this wanton bloodthirstiness stated that there were some Arabs who were a cut above the common herd of barbarous Muslims. They always placed Hamed bin Muhammad in that category.

In July 1874 Tippu Tip met a raiding party led by Mwinyi Dagumbi and Mtagamoyo. The Nyangwe leaders gave a hearty welcome to their illustrious compatriot and Tippu Tip was no less delighted to see them. It was from these two prize rogues that he received his first news from the coast in over three years. Momentous events had taken place in his absence. Sultan Majid had died and been replaced by his brother Barghash. In 1872 a fierce cyclone had carved its way across Zanzibar—a unique event in the island's history—killing, destroying, uprooting and quite upsetting the government's precarious economy. Taking advantage of Barghash's weakened position the British had, on 5th June 1873, forced him to sign a treaty outlawing the slave trade from his dominions. This was the turning point in the long war against slavery in East Africa. The news would have gladdened the heart of slavery's most active opponent but he had died five weeks before on the shore of Lake Bangweulu. To Livingstone's death on 1st May and the signing of the Frere Treaty on 5th June we may add another event to make up a trilogy of significant dates in the year 1873: on 24th March Captain Verney Lovett Cameron set out from the east coast port of Bagamoyo on what was to be the first trans-continental journey through Africa to be completed by a European.

Did Tippu Tip see the writing on the wall? Probably not. He was just approaching the zenith of his power and influence. With large slave armies at his command, with vassal chiefs paying him tribute, with a fortune in ivory in his store houses and more coming in daily, with the universal respect of all the other Zanzibari traders in the interior, he might well feel secure. The cloud on the horizon was no bigger than a man's hand; to Tippu Tip it did not appear ominous. When Cameron arrived in his camp a few weeks later Hamed showed the explorer his customary courtesy and even postponed a planned visit to Kasongo to travel with Cameron and see him safely on his way into the Congo basin.

His duty as host done, Tippu Tip resumed his journey to Kasongo. This was a village up-river from Nyangwe where the Arabs had established a trading depot. His countrymen welcomed the great adventurer with open arms. They were in trouble due to shortage of food, hostility of the local people and defection of slaves and porters. They looked to Tippu Tip to set all to rights. One answer sufficed for all the problems. A series of short campaigns made up the deficiency of slaves, brought the locals to a more accommodating frame of mind and brought food in abundance to Kasongo. From this time onward the Zanzibaris trading throughout this region recognised Tippu Tip as their leader.

Hamed bin Muhammad el Murjebi was now in all but name an emperor. Through his agents and vassals he controlled an area of some 250,000 square miles. His realm extended from Lake Tanganyika in the east to the Lubilash river in the west, from Katanga in the south to the middle reaches of the Lualaba in the north. Throughout this area he made and un-made chiefs, he controlled the trade in ivory and the hunting of elephants, his fiat ran for the establishment of peace or the declaration of war, he fixed the price of ivory and other goods, he supervised the building of fortified depots and he encouraged the spread of Islam.

In October 1876 Tippu Tip came face to face with a man who was his equal in ruthlessness, energy, determination, bravery and guile. Perhaps he was Tippu Tip's superior in perfidy, egoism and ingratitude—it is a matter of opinion. Henry Morton Stanley was halfway through one of the most momentous journeys in history. The bustling, bumptious, forceful and ambitious young Welshman, the successful journalist, the finder of the great Livingstone, left Britain in the middle of 1874 on a wave of sentiment and enthusiasm inspired by the news of Livingstone's death. 'The work of England for Africa must henceforth begin in earnest where Livingstone left it off,' wrote

The Times, and Stanley was in the van of those Englishmen who dedicated themselves to the memory of the great explorer and to Africa. Entering the continent with the largest and most lavishly equipped caravan yet to travel in Africa under European leadership, Stanley devoted two years to tying up the few geographical loose ends concerned with the source of the White Nile and the Great Lakes system. A steel boat carried in sections was assembled first on Lake Victoria and subsequently on Lake Tanganyika and those two inland seas were accurately mapped for the first time.

There remained only the problem which Livingstone had been working on at the time of his death—the Lualaba and its possible connection with the Nile or Congo system. It was in quest of the solution to this problem that Stanley came to Kasongo on 18th October 1876. For the next two months his story was intimately bound up with that of Tippu Tip.

The explorer was welcomed and provided with a house. Tippu Tip ordered that every attention should be paid to the comfort of Stanley and his men. But Stanley wanted more than hospitality. On his third evening at Kasongo he told the Arab what was on his mind. They were seated on rugs and cushions in Tippu Tip's house. The brief tropical dusk had passed and lamps guttered about the room. The small company had supped and were discussing the difficulties earlier explorers had experienced. According to Stanley's account Tippu Tip explained that he had offered to hire his services to Cameron for a trip down the Lualaba:

' "I suppose, Tippu-Tib [*sic*]," I said, "having offered the other white man your assistance, you would have no objections to offer it to me for the same sum?"

' "I don't know about that," he replied, with a smile. "I have not many people with me now. Many are at Imbarri, others are trading in Manyema."

' "How many men have you with you?"

' "Perhaps three hundred—or say two hundred and fifty."

' "That number would be a grand escort, amply sufficient, if well managed, to ensure perfect protection."

' "Yes, united with your party, it would be a very strong force, but how would it be when I returned alone? The natives would say, seeing only my little force, 'These people have been fighting—half of them are killed, because they have no ivory with them; let us finish them!' I know, my friend, these savages very well, and I tell you that that would be their way of thinking."

' "But, my friend," said I, "think how it would be with me. with all the continent before me, and only protected by my little band!"

' "Ah, yes! if you Wasungu (white men) are desirous of throwing away your lives, it is no reason we Arabs should. We travel little by little to get ivory and slaves, and are years about it—it is now nine years since I left Zanzibar— but you white men only look for rivers and lakes and mountains, and you spend your lives for no reason, and to no purpose. Look at that old man who died in Bisa! What did he seek year after year, until he became so old that he could not travel? He had no money, for he never gave any of us anything, he bought no ivory or slaves, yet he travelled farther than any of us, and for what?" '

So the discussion went on far into the night until Tippu Tip announced that he would sleep on the problem and give his answer in the morning. And in the morning he agreed to accompany Stanley's party with 140 armed men.

This decision was crucial for the ultimate success of the expedition. Kasongo was almost on the edge of the Congo forest into which few strangers dared to venture. The forest was dense and reputedly peopled by inhospitable cannibals. The river was difficult to negotiate and its course unknown. Both Livingstone and Cameron had been refused assistance by Mwinyi Dugumbi when they wished to travel down the river. Africans and Arabs alike shrank from committing themselves to that dripping, green hell. Even Stanley and his European colleagues debated long their best course of action; whether they should attempt the river route or whether they should strike due west, as Cameron had done, and thus skirt the forest.

Tippu Tip's kinsmen and friends both at Kasongo and Nyangwe tried hard to dissuade him from the enterprise. 'You have left your work to follow this European without knowing where he is going.' 'What, going with a European, have you lost your senses?' 'You're mad, will you then become a European?' 'You've not need. You have your stock of ivory, why then follow an Unbeliever?' Tippu Tip's reaction was more a retort than an answer, 'Maybe I am mad, and you are sensible. Nevertheless, keep to your own affairs.'

But why did he decide to accompany Stanley on what he clearly believed to be a hazardous and reckless venture? Stanley believed that the Arab was lured by the 5,000 dollars he promised to pay him, but it is doubtful whether this figure can have impressed the great trader much.* In part Hamed bin Muhammad was responding to the challenge of the unknown, for he was at heart an adventurer. But he was even more a businessman. The possibility of opening up new elephant-hunting grounds was never far from his thoughts and acted as a stimulus on this occasion. The forest harboured large herds of elephant and, reputedly, people who did not know the value of tusks. Tippu Tip might therefore discharge his duty to the European and do himself a bit of good at the same time. When on 5th November his party linked up with Stanley's it contained an extra 300 men, who were to accompany the expedition until fruitful grounds for raiding, trading or hunting were en-

---

* There is complete disagreement between the accounts of Stanley and Tippu Tip as to the exact terms of the contract agreed between them. Stanley mentions the figure of 5,000 dollars, Tippu Tip quotes 7,000 dollars as the sum owed. Stanley avers that part of this sum was paid to Tippu Tip before his defection. The Arab complained that he never received a penny. Faced with the testimony of two such rogues it is difficult to decide which is likely to be closer to the truth. My inclination is to place more reliance on Tippu Tip's account. 5,000 or 7,000 dollars can have meant little to him and for all he knew he stood to lose more than he might gain from the expedition. It was easy for Stanley, writing later in the comfort of his English study, to complain in his book about Tippu Tip's perfidy and to impress upon his eager readers that to all the other hardships of his journey was that of having to rely on treacherous, Muslim slavers. If Stanley believed Tippu Tip to be as scheming and unreliable as he said, it is difficult to see why he took the Arab with him on another Congo journey in 1887.

countered. Whatever Tippu Tip's motives may have been Stanley was in no doubt about his good fortune in securing the services of the Arab. He wrote in his diary:

'Tippu-Tib is the most dashing and adventurous Arab that has ever entered Africa and to ensure success in this exploration I could not have done better than to have secured his aid in exploring a dangerous country. Few tribes will care to dispute our passage now. I look forward in strong hopes to do valuable explorations.'

That journey was the worst Tippu Tip ever made. Whether travelling along the river in Stanley's boat or in stolen canoes or hacking through the jungle, the going was uncomfortable and full of hazards. By land the complaining porters and gunmen had to cut out every step of the way through bushes, creepers and dead trees. As well as these obstacles they were continually impeded by slippery mud and rotting vegetation underfoot. They tripped and slithered and swore and got in each other's way as they tried to follow the path in the perpetual dim, green, shadowy twilight. Sometimes they were lucky if they had covered three miles at the end of a gruelling day's march. Every member of the expedition put the blame on the Englishman and soon they were calling the Congo jungle, 'the Forest of the Infidel'.

Conditions were scarcely better on the river. To the hazards of rocks, rapids and crocodiles was added the uncertainty of their reception by the African communities living on the banks and islands. Most of the Africans the explorers met were terrified and took to the forest. This made it easy to obtain canoes but difficult to bargain for food. At other times the newcomers were assailed by showers of poisoned arrows as they approached a settlement.

Thus the expedition continued for six weeks. For most of this time Tippu Tip led the larger land party while Stanley travelled down the river, making much faster progress but frequently chafing at the delays caused by Tippu Tip's men who were always late reaching rendezvous points. Considering the difficulties faced by the land party Stanley's irritation was, to say the least, unreasonable. But Tippu Tip now had another, and worse, enemy to face—smallpox. From 11th December the dreadful disease claimed fresh victims every day. Having caught and recovered from smallpox as a young man Tippu Tip had no fear of it but the epidemic caused panic among his followers.

On 22nd December Tippu Tip announced that he and his men could go no further. There remained eleven days of his contract to serve but, having reached a point two hundred and fifty miles down river from Nyangwe the Arab believed that he had discharged his obligations in accordance with the spirit if not the letter of the law. Stanley was now well provided with canoes and would proceed quicker without the land party. Tippu Tip's force was already depleted by disease, accident and war. He dared not go any further. He did not mention another reason why he wished to be rid of the explorer's party: he had heard that along the lower Lomami ivory was to be had for a song.

As soon as Stanley's men heard that the ways of the Englishman and the Arab were to divide, they mutinied. 'If Hamed bin Muhammad returns we return too; we're not going to a foreign place. Anyway we signed on at the coast for two years, and it is already two and a half years. If Hamed returns we insist on returning too.' Once again Stanley was completely in Tippu Tip's hands—a humiliating experience for a man of his pride and ambition. He begged Hamed to reason with the strikers. Hamed agreed, but only by dint of long argument, cajoling, bullying, threatening and bribing did he succeed in returning Stanley's men to their loyalty.

The parting seems to have been amicable enough; on Christmas Day the expedition stopped for dances, races and festivities and on the following day Tippu Tip gave a farewell banquet to Stanley's party. There was an exchange of presents between the two leaders and on 27th December Stanley and his followers set off alone. A little over seven months later he reached the west coast with a much depleted party, having successfully charted the course of the Congo and accomplished one of the most astounding feats of geographical discovery in the history of exploration. No sooner had he recovered and set off on a restful sea voyage back to England than he began to accuse Tippu Tip—the man to whom above all others he owed the success of his expedition—of treachery, deceit and breach of contract.

By this time Tippu Tip was back at Kasongo. The Lomami region had yielded up cheap ivory in abundance:

'When I reached Lomami, my four frasila of copper yielded 200 frasila of ivory. I made armlets (bangles), three pounds of copper to five bangles, and two bangles for a tusk. In a month our trading was finished . . . At this time the locals did not use ivory as exchange. They hunted elephant and ate the meat but used the tusks in their homes for a stockade. With others they made pestles and mortars for their cooking bananas . . . Others they made into flutes, and some they threw into the bush where they were eaten by animals, such as rats.Others rotted, giving off a stench as they decomposed.'

So the Congo trip, though unpleasant, was eventually from Tippu Tip's point of view, worthwhile.

Now he was at the height of his power and fame. There was no other man in East and Central Africa who enjoyed a comparable reputation. In business there was no beating about the bush; it was always 'take it or leave it', and in warfare, 'unconditional surrender' was the basis of his terms to all enemies who sued for peace. His power was sung around most camp fires, from the East Coast to Stanley Pool on the Congo. His very name was sufficient to strike terror into the hearts of all who were liable to attack.

Meanwhile the journeys of Cameron and Stanley were exciting great interest in Europe. Companies were founded for the further exploration and exploitation of the Congo basin. While the King of Manyemaland lorded over thousands of subjects the King of the Belgians was planning the creation of a Central African empire. As the fateful decade of the 1880s dawned more and more white men—traders, missionaries, explorers and hunters—were entering the continent from east and west. For those who had eyes to see, the cloud no bigger than a man's hand was spreading, darkening and advancing.

5

*Every pound weight has cost the life of a man, woman or child; for
every five pounds a hut has been burned; for every two tusks a village
has been destroyed; every twenty tusks have been obtained at the price
of a district with all its people, villages and plantations.'*

—H. M. Stanley

Black and White Ivory

In 1839 human greed achieved something which had defied
human enterprise and adventurousness for eighteen centuries.
An Egyptian expedition, fired by the prospect of reaching a
vast new area of potential ivory and slave trading, broke
through the Sudd, the extensive area of fifteen-foot high
papyrus swamp and floating vegetation which blocks the course
of the White Nile south of the Sobat junction. Not since the
time of the Emperor Nero's unsuccessful venture around A.D. 60
had this formidable feat been attempted. Its success opened an
enormous 'hidden' area of Africa and revived interest in the
search for the Nile source. For the next fifty years explorers,
adventurers, slavers, government agents, ivory traders and
missionaries poured into the southern Sudan and created havoc.

What Zanzibar was to the commercial life of East and Central
Africa Khartoum was to the Sudan.

'Each year, when the north winds begin to blow at Khartoum,
towards the middle of November, an expedition of a dozen
boats ascends the White Nile as far as 4.30' Lat. north . . .
These boats bring back annually about 400 quintals of ivory,
which brought to Cairo represents a value of approximately
100,000 francs.* To procure this ivory they give beads
whose value does certainly not exceed 1,000 francs.'

---

* One quintal was equivalent to about 100 lb.

But while Zanzibar was dominated by Arab traders and Indian banyans the great ivory entrepôt at the junction of the Blue and White Niles was a truly cosmopolitan centre. The exploitation of the Sudan was part of an imperial thrust southwards initiated by the Egyptian ruler Muhammad Ali, in 1820–21. Khartoum grew rapidly from a military H.Q. to an administrative capital. The government encouraged consuls and merchants of all nations—Austrians, Greeks, Turks, Germans, Englishmen, Ethiopians, Arabs—to establish themselves in the new city and to assist in the work of opening up the area further south.

Khartoum was like a boom town no less remarkable than the mushrooming gold mining centres of California. Wealthy merchants were borne through its streets in their carriages. Penniless adventurers sought backers for desperate trips up the Nile which would make their fortunes. Here prosperous ivory dealers such as the Maltese Andrea de Bono and the Greek Alaro had their beautiful houses, furnished in luxurious and opulent taste. Here, in this desert township at the world's end, were European shops where 'guns, ready-made clothes, wines, Bass's Ale, groceries, hardware, and other goods were available'. Here Muslim mosques stood shoulder to shoulder with Coptic and Protestant churches and a Roman Catholic mission station.

It was this multi-national community which, in its pursuit of ivory, opened up the upper Nile region. Giovanni Miani, a Venetian, explored the Bahr el-Ghazal, penetrated deep into modern Uganda and brought back stories of rivers that flowed westwards (tributaries of the Congo). Jules Poncet reached the fabulous elephant country west of the Bahr el-Jebel (later to go down in ivory-hunting history as the Lado Enclave—*see* Chapter 7). Piaggia, another Italian, reached the edge of the Congo forest in 1862. By then de Bono already had a large depot at Faloro, between the modern Ugandan towns of Gulu and Rhino Camp. 'At Faloro,' James Grant reported, 'there were upwards of a hundred men of every caste and colour . . . There were only one or two European countenances. Curly locks were exceptional and wool predominated. They were adventurers without a home.' Soon after Samuel Baker officially discovered and named Lake Albert, in 1864, Romolo Gessi established himself on its shores and began a lively trade in fine tusks. At Gondokoro Baker found a trading settlement of over 600 lawless men seemingly occupied in nothing but drinking, quarrelling and shooting off their guns without provocation: he could only describe the place as 'a perfect hell'.

In fact, everything about the ivory/slave trade in the north was diabolical. The Khartoumers had a contempt for the human and animal inhabitants of the southern Sudan which was total. If they were hard men to begin with, their journey through the Sudd stripped from them any refinements of civilisation and humanity. In this stinking, tangled mass of rotting vegetation which, at times, was as big as England, only the mosquitoes flourished. Men needed the incentive of great wealth to undertake a voyage on which disease, starvation and death were their most familiar companions. Once safely through the barrier of the Sudd they used every means available to obtain the maximum amount of ivory and then filled every vacant space in their boats with slaves.

In the early days of this trade there was little violence. The newcomers were dependent upon the goodwill and knowledge of the locals. The riverain Cic and Dinka gladly exchanged tusks for beads with the Khartoumers, as John Petherick, one of the first British travellers in the Sudan, reported:

'The only article of importance offered for trade is Ivory, which is bartered for various kinds of beads, cowries and occasionally from one to four or five pairs of Copper Bracelets. The beads most in demand are large white round beads, known in commerce as "Bered" or "Pidgeons' [sic] Eggs", from two to three hundred being given for a tusk according to the size thereof—the latter being the value of a fine tusk weighing one hundredweight or upwards. The value of the tusk having been decided as regards the "Bered", the final puchase is easily concluded, as a pair or two of copper bracelets, and small quantities of different sorts of small beads viz. Blue, Black, White, Red and Green, the whole amounting to 3 or 4 lbs weight, and a 1000 or 2 cowrie shells are deemed ample payment.

'The purchase concluded and the Beads consigned it is different with regard to the ivory. Some 8 or 12 porters who had brought the ivory to market immediately sieze it and do not give it up until they each receive a "Bacjshish" of Beads for their trouble, when the purchaser's men take hold of one extremity, and the negroes hold fast the other end of the tusk, and a good-humoured struggle commences for the possession thereof, which is often only obtained by pelting off the Negroes with beads, when after a moderate shower amidst hearty laughter they abandon the contest to collect the beads and the purchase is concluded.'

But soon the supplies of elephants close to the Nile were exhausted and the demand for beads was satisfied. Then the mask of friendship was cast aside. The Khartoumers mounted their own expeditions, either ignoring their previous trade partners or arming them with guns and persuading them to raid their neighbours. Samuel Baker has left us with a vivid picture of how this 'commerce' worked:

'The vessels sail about December, and on arrival at the desired locality, the party disembark and proceed into the interior, until they arrive at the village of some negro chief, with whom they establish an intimacy. Charmed with his new friends, the power of whose weapons he acknowledges, the negro chief does not neglect the opportunity of seeking their alliance to attack a hostile neighbour. Marching throughout the night, guided by their negro hosts, they bivouac within an hour's march of the unsuspecting village doomed to an attack about half an hour before break of day. The time arrives, and quietly surrounding the village while its occupants are still sleeping, they fire the grass huts in all directions, and pour volleys of musketry through the flaming thatch. Panic-stricken, the unfortunate victims rush from their burning dwellings, and the men are shot down like pheasants in a battue, while the women and children, bewildered in the danger and confusion, are kidnapped and secured. The herds of cattle, still within their kraal or "zareeba", are easily disposed of, and are driven off with great rejoicing, as the prize of victory. The women and children are then fastened together, the former secured in an instrument called a shéba, made of a forked pole, the neck of the prisoner fitting into the fork, secured by a cross piece lashed behind, while the wrists, brought together in advance of the body, are tied to the pole. The children are then fastened by their necks with a rope attached to the women, and thus form a living chain, in which order they are marched to the head-quarters in company with the captured herds.

'This is the commencement of business: should there be ivory in any of the huts not destroyed by the fire, it is appropriated; a general plunder takes place. The trader's party dig up the floors of the huts to search for iron hoes, which are generally thus concealed, as the greatest treasure of the negroes; the granaries are overturned and wantonly destroyed, and the hands are cut off the bodies of the slain the more easily to detach the copper or iron bracelets that are usually worn. With this booty the *traders* return to their negro ally: they have thrashed and discomfited his enemy, which delights him; they present him with thirty or forty head of cattle, which intoxicates him with joy, and a present of a pretty little captive girl of about fourteen completes his happiness.

'But business has only commenced. The negro covets cattle, and the trader has now captured perhaps 2,000 head. They are to be had for ivory, and shortly the tusks appear. Ivory is daily brought into camp in exchange for cattle, a tusk for a cow, according to size—a profitable business, as the cows have cost nothing. The trade proves brisk; but still there remain some little customs to be observed—some slight formalities, well understood by the White Nile trade. The slaves and two-thirds of the captured cattle belong to the trader, but his men claim as their perquisite one-third of the stolen animals. These having been divided, the slaves are put up to public auction among the men, who purchase such as they require; the amount being entered on the papers (serki) of the purchasers, to be reckoned against their wages. To avoid the exposure, should the document fall into the hands of the Government or European consuls, the amount is not entered as for the purchase of a slave, but is divided for fictitious supplies—thus, should a slave be purchased for 1,000 piastres, that amount would appear on the document somewhat as follows:

Soap	50 Piastres
Tarboash (cap)	100
Araki	150
Shoes	200
Cotton Cloth	500
	1,000

'The slaves sold to the men are constantly being changed and resold among themselves; but should the relatives of the kidnapped women and children wish to ransom them, the trader takes them from his men, cancels the amount of purchase, and restores them to their relations for a certain number of elephants' tusks, as may be agreed upon. Should any slave attempt to escape, she is punished either by brutal flogging, or shot or hanged, as a warning to others.

'An attack or razzia, such as described, generally leads to a quarrel with the negro ally, who in his turn is murdered and plundered by the trader—his women and children naturally becoming slaves.

'A good season for a party of a hundred and fifty men should produce about 20,000 lbs of ivory, valued at Khartoum at £4,000. The men being paid in slaves, the wages should be *nil*, and there should be a surplus of four or five hundred slaves for the trader's own profit—worth on an average five to six pounds each.

'The boats are accordingly packed with a human cargo, and a portion of the trader's men accompany them to the Soudan, while the remainder of the party form a camp or settlement in the country they have adopted, and industriously plunder, massacre, and enslave, until their master's return with boats from Khartoum in the following season, by which time they are supposed to have a cargo of slaves and ivory ready for shipment.'

Chaos and violence spread rapidly as the newcomers deliberately encouraged tribal rivalries and extended their activities further and further from the river. Tracks and camps soon covered much of the southern Sudan and the traders had to establish permanent bases or *zeribas*. A zeriba might be very large—a stockaded area covering many acres, containing huts for all the men, night bomas for the cattle, as well as special buildings for storing the ivory and ammunition and an area for concluding deals with local rulers who brought in tusks. As early as 1856 the Frenchman, A. de Malzac, had already established such a zeriba eight days' march from the Nile. He adorned its stockade with the heads of his victims, and instilled such terror into the people that whole tribes fled from the area. It is hardly surprising that after his first season de Malzac had to employ 500 porters to carry his ivory to the waiting steamers on the Nile. Nor is it surprising that an Austrian diplomat reported to his superiors, 'there are no longer merchants, but only slavers and robbers on the White Nile'.

It is not uncommon in commercial enterprises that those who take the greatest risks and do the dirtiest work secure the smallest share of the rewards, and this was often the case in the Sudanic ivory trade. Competition grew, African allies made greater demands, more men and ammunition were required to gain the same amount of ivory. As the risk of failure increased so did the interest rates of the moneylenders in Khartoum. Financial support had never been cheap but now the cost of money rose from 36% to 60% and even 80%. Commercial success was more important than ever. The traders became desperate, assuming the savagery and cunning of leopards in their determination to make each expedition pay. So the violence and rapacity increased and more than one merchant was drawn into the maelstrom of death which he and his kind had set in motion. Ivory seekers needed to be constantly on their guard against the sudden raid, the treachery of an ally and the poisoned arrow loosed in desperation by a defeated foe.

Partly for these reasons and partly as a result of the deliberate policy of the Egyptian government, which did not like to see the lion's share of commercial profit falling to aliens, the number of Europeans operating in the Sudan gradually dwindled. Turks, Egyptians and Arabs were left to run the zeribas. The most successful of them was al-Zubair Rahma Mansur. A Ja'li Arab from a village on the Nile, he joined his first expedition to the Bahr-el-Ghazal in 1856 at the age of 25. Events on that journey soon took a violent and exciting turn:

'. . . there had passed but a few months when the natives rose against the merchants, envying them their possessions . . . they collected from all directions and stormed the zeribas, killing some of the merchants and carrying off their goods as trophies. They also attacked the zeriba of Ali Amuri (Zubair's leader), but I led his men and opened fire on the savages, routing them and killing large numbers: Praise be to God, the High, the Mighty. When the merchants heard of my success they flocked round, and I became in high estimation with them, so that the natives of the country were afraid and did not dare to renew their attack. My friend Ali Amuri, seeing that I was the cause of his escape, loved me exceedingly and gave me a share in his profits, to wit one tenth of all his ivory.'

We do not need to take Zubair at his own valuation to recognise him as a man courageous, resourceful and ruthless. He was soon leading his own expeditions and penetrating further south and west than any of his contemporaries. He married a daughter of the powerful Azande chief Tikima and by alliance and conquest carved out for himself a kingdom the size of France. His principal zeriba, Deim Zubair, housed thousands of armed followers and large ivory storehouses. From here raiding parties set out and it was to Deim Zubair that tribute was brought from vassal chiefs in the form of tusks. The pattern was, in fact, almost identical to that established by Tippu Tip and his confrères in the Congo.

In 1869 Khedive Ismail of Egypt decided that Zubair was too powerful and sent agents to assume command of the Bahr el-Ghazal. Several traders submitted to Muhammad al-Hilali but others preferred to see how Zubair would react. The great trader respectfully declined to lay down his authority. Two years of intrigue and argument followed during which Hilali (who was called Billali in Zubair's narrative) used every stratagem to win over Zubair's allies. When he felt himself strong enough the Khedive's agent launched an attack on Deim Zubair, being careful to choose a time when the proprietor was some days' journey away from his base. When Zubair heard the news he hurried home, completing

'. . . in thirty six hours a journey that ordinarily requires three whole days. But I was too late, for I discovered that Billali had privily despatched some men who had set fire to the town. Nothing was left over from the havoc of the fire, but as fate had decreed, I had hidden my ammunition in the ground, and this was unharmed by the flames. As for the place itself there was neither fosse nor rampart, with which to repel the hosts of my enemy: and, indeed, what availed they, seeing that I had but five hundred and twenty three men [he had dispersed most of his force to other garrisons to guard against sudden attack by Hilali]? Then news was brought me that Billali proposed to attack me in the twilight before the dawn, so I hastily divided my forces into five divisions, which were placed in the town in such a way as would most incommode the enemy. At the ninth hour of the day Billali with a force of nearly four thousand men, armed with ten dozen rounds of ammunition a man—as I discovered later from a list that came into my possession—appeared in the neighbourhood. Then my cousin came to me and said that he had seen my men and lo! their foreheads were bedewed with perspiration by reason of the excess of fear that had overcome them: so I went to my men, and upbraided them for the fear that they endured, and I took of the sheep which were with me, and I slaughtered of them that thereby my men might eat and be heartened. Next I destroyed six cantars (about 3,000 lbs) of ivory, that it might not be a trophy for the foe, and went to my tent with sorrow in my heart for the doom that I saw hanging over my friends and relations. . . .(The battle began soon after this.) Then, indeed, did a kind of madness possess my men, and we, who were so few, hurled ourselves upon the foe who were so many: and no sooner had we attacked than lo! we found ourselves in the midst of the foe, fighting with swords, revolvers, sticks and even the palms of our hands. Then Musa wad el Haj, one of my commanders, fell on the flank of the enemy, and soon all was confusion, while Billali vainly shouted first this command and then that. In the end, finding that defeat would be his portion, Billali fled in the direction of Dar Mufio, while we released from their sheibas the prisoners whom he had brought. The next day . . . there came . . . Rabeh, who overtook Billali at Deim Gugu, near the country of Mufio, and killed him.'

The Khedive was left with little alternative but to reach an accommodation with Zubair. He recognised the *de facto* ruler as his governor of Bahr el-Ghazal Province in return for annual tribute of £15,000 worth of ivory (a payment which made little impression on Zubair's astonishing ivory stocks). With his prestige thus enhanced Zubair continued his career of conquest. Without sanction from Cairo he overran the ancient sultanate of Darfur to the north and harried the neighbouring state of Wadai. Ismael honoured Zubair with the title of Pasha for this feat but he was growing increasingly anxious about his over-mighty subject. Stories reached him daily of his governor's latest conquests, of the regal splendour with which he surrounded himself in the rebuilt Deim Zubair, of his large harem and of his seventy sons, of the boatloads of ivory he sent annually to Khartoum, of the modern rifles with which he equipped his men, and of the enormous bribes with which he neutralized the loyalty of the Khedive's agents. In 1876 Ismael inveigled Zubair Pasha into paying a visit to Cairo. Once in the capital and separated from his armed retainers Zubair was honourably detained. There he was destined to remain for many years. Impotent, he watched the empire he had built up fall apart, saw the Mahdist revolt sweep across the Sudan and close the trade routes along which his ivory had once flowed. Perhaps he heard Charles Gordon's *cri du coeur* from Khartoum: 'As for Zubair, I wish with all my heart he was here. He alone can ride the Sudan horse, and if they do not send him I am sentenced to penal servitude for my life up here.'

During the years of Zubair's ascendancy an increasing number of Europeans visited the Sudan. It was partly as a result of their reports and the pressures brought to bear by representatives of their governments at Cairo and Constantinople that Ismael attempted to make a reality of Egyptian rule in the Sudan. What concerned the white men most was the slave trade but there were many who were appalled at the carnage of elephants. Samuel Baker recorded his disgust at the wholesale slaughter of animals provoked by the ivory trade:

'The great elephant hunting season is in January, when the high prairies are parched and reduced to straw. At such a time, should a large herd of animals be discovered, the natives

The quarry – an African bush elephant

(*Photograph by Simon Trevor; copyright Bruce Coleman Ltd*)

The elephant as seen by rock painters of
the Eastern Desert over 8000 years ago

'Flocks of elephants that lay waste whole forests' – an African scene as envisaged by a 17th century European artist

John Owen, a District Commissioner in the Torit area
of the Sudan, showing assistants how to remove the
tusks from a dead rogue elephant

(Copyright Radio Times Hulton Picture Library)

A 17th century Congolese carver made this salt cellar for one of the Portuguese conquerors

(*Copyright British Museum*)

An exquisite comb fashioned by a Congolese craftsman

(*Copyright British Museum*)

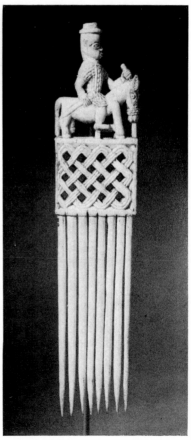

African elephant hunters, according to a 16th century European artist

(Copyright Radio Times Hulton Picture Library)

Ethiopians hunting elephant

(*Mary Evans Picture Library*)

Cornwallis Harris' impressions of elephant hunting in South Africa in the 1830s. Note the severely wounded animal – a victim of early, unscientific hunting methods.

(Photograph by courtesy of British Museum Camera Press)

W G HARRIS

Tippu Tip

An ivory dealer from Gabon
(*Mary Evans Picture Library*)

Boer hunters c. 1880

(Copyright Radio Times Hulton Picture Library)

Emin Pasha with some of his ivory

(Mary Evans Picture Library)

Colesberg declines being mounted

Riding out the best Bull Elephant

Hazards of the chase, according to Gordon Cumming

A London ivory warehouse in the 1890s

of the entire district collect together to the number of perhaps a thousand men; surrounding the elephants by embracing a considerable tract of country they fire the grass at a given signal. In a few minutes the unconscious elephants are surrounded by a circle of fire, which, however distant, must eventually close in upon them. The men advance with the fire, which rages to the height of twenty or thirty feet. At length the elephants, alarmed by the volumes of smoke and the roaring of the flames, mingled with the shouts of the hunters, attempt an escape. They are hemmed in on every side—wherever they rush, they are met by an impassable barrier of flames and smoke, so stifling, that they are forced to retreat. Meanwhile the fatal circle is decreasing; buffaloes and antelopes, likewise doomed to a horrible fate, crowd panic-stricken to the centre of the encircled ring, and the raging fire sweeps over all. Burnt, and blinded by fire and smoke, the animals are now attacked by the savage crowd of hunters, excited by the helplessness of the unfortunate elephants thus miserably sacrificed, and they fall under countless spears. This destructive method of hunting, ruins the game of that part of Africa, and so scarce are the antelopes, that, in a day's journey, a dozen head are seldom seen in the open prairie.'

Samuel White Baker was a tough, burly, self-assured, wealthy Englishman with a passion for guns, who had already spent several years as a colonist in Ceylon. Having turned thousands of acres of jungle into flourishing plantations and shot every species of animal on the island he tired of Ceylon and sought fresh challenges. Africa offered him two such challenges, the Nile and the elephant. Baker and his equally hardy wife made two visits to Africa: from 1861 to 1865 he explored the Nile sources, becoming the first white man to reach Lake Albert, and from 1869 to 1873 he was employed by the Khedive as Governor-general of Equatoria, a vast, ill-defined region of the southern Sudan to the south of Bahr el-Ghazal province.

Throughout his African travels Baker never missed an opportunity of hunting elephants. He encountered his first beasts on the banks of the Atbara in northern Ethiopia (some 600 miles or more from the nearest herd of elephants today) and was as excited by the hunting techniques of the local 'braves' as he was at the prospect of bagging his own ivory. The *aggaggeers* pursued their quarry on horseback and were armed only with exceedingly sharp swords. Hunting in packs of four it was their object to distract the chosen elephant with feints and rushes while one of their number rode in close enough to slash the sinews of the animal's back legs. This done the immobilised beast was left to bleed to death while the *aggaggeers* went in search of another prey. Baker admired the bravery of these men, several of whom were maimed or killed by elephants or by chance blows from their own vicious weapons.

Baker's own armoury of weapons was scarcely less formidable. Chief among his elephant guns was a massive- single-barrelled Holland which the Arabs called *Jenna el-Mootfah* (child of a cannon) and which he nicknamed the 'baby'. It fired a half pound explosive shell which had a devastating effect, as Baker discovered when he examined the carcase of the first elephant he shot with it:

'. . . it had entered the flank on the right side, breaking the rib upon which it had exploded; it had then passed through the stomach and the lower portion of the lungs, both of which were terribly shattered, and breaking one of the fore-ribs on the left side, it had lodged beneath the skin of the shoulder. This was irresistible work, and the elephant had evidently dropped in a few minutes after having received the shell.'

The 'baby' had a fairly devastating effect on the firer also. Loaded with ten drachms of powder, its recoil could be guaranteed to knock even a man of Baker's physique off his feet. It is scarcely surprising that throughout his African travels he only used the 'baby' about twenty times.

For some of his other guns the hunter made his own bullets, to a personally proved formula. He mixed one part of mercury with twelve parts of molten lead and poured the amalgam into conical moulds. When these bullets were propelled by seven drachms of powder they had considerable penetrative power. The first elephant which Baker claimed with one of these bullets he hit in the centre of the forehead. The bullet penetrated the skull, passed through the brain, emerged from the back of the skull and finally buried itself in the spine between the shoulders. After the smaller and less energetic elephants of Ceylon, Baker found the African variety difficult to shoot accurately at close range. He was rarely able to position himself for the frontal shot and found often that when he did use this shot even his formidable bullets failed to penetrate the animal's thick skull.

Although Baker accumulated hundreds of tusks during his years in the Sudan he was always more interested in hunting for its own sake than in ivory. On the Uganda border in 1863 he adopted the Arab custom of hunting on horseback. This did not prove an unmitigated success largely because Baker underestimated the speed and endurance of an angry elephant:

'Riding along the open plain I at length arrived within about fifty yards of the bull, when he slowly turned. Reining "Tétel" up, I immediately fired a steady shot at the shoulder with the Reilly No. 10: for a moment he fell upon his knees, but, recovering with wonderful quickness, he was in full charge upon me . . . away I went up the inclination to my right, the spurs hard at work, and the elephant screaming with rage, *gaining* on me. My horse felt as though made of wood, and clumsily rode along in a sort of cow-gallop; in vain I dug the spurs into his flanks, and urged him by rein and voice; not an extra stride could I get out of him, and he reeled along as though thoroughly exhausted, plunging in and out of the buffalo holes instead of jumping them . . . I kept looking round, thinking that the elephant would give in: we had been running for nearly half a mile, and the brute was overhauling me so fast that he was within ten or twelve yards of the horse's tail, with his trunk stretched out to catch him. Screaming like the whistle of an engine, he fortunately so frightened the horse that he went his best, though badly, and I turned him suddenly down the hill and doubled back like a hare. The elephant turned up the hill, and entering the jungle he relinquished the chase, when another hundred yards' run would have bagged me.'

Baker found that as he travelled south he encountered more

elephants with large tusks, a sure sign that the relentless pursuit of ivory by the Khartoumers was beginning to take its predestined toll. Yet, however much he despised the ivory and slave traders Baker, like white travellers in East and Central Africa, was forced to rely on them for practical assistance. Southwards from Gondokoro the Bakers accompanied Ibrahim, the representative of a Circassian trader named Aga. The Europeans paid well for Ibrahim's aid and Baker helped his host to locate and hunt elephants. The explorers would never have reached their objective (Lake Albert) without the Turk's assistance but this did not make it easy for Baker to accept reliance on the accursed slavers:

'It is remarkably pleasant! travelling in the vicinity of the traders; they convert every country into a wasp's nest— they have neither plan of action nor determination, and I, being unfortunately dependent upon their movements, am more like a donkey than an explorer, that is saddled and ridden away at a moment's notice.'

Doubtless Ibrahim had no relish for the partnership either. Florence Baker fell ill and slowed the progress of the caravan; her husband was always protesting about Ibrahim's slave and cattle raids. But the Turk was bound by laws of hospitality more powerful than the dictates of commercial convenience and he eventually had reason to thank Baker for persuading him to trek far to the south. When they reached the kingdom of Bunyoro they found a state abounding in ivory and almost untouched by commerce. Few traders had ever reached Bunyoro from the north and the Zanzibaris who would dearly have loved to trade with the Banyoro were prevented from doing so by the mighty Mutesa, King of Buganda, a rival state on the northern shore of Lake Victoria. Kamurasi, the ruler, was, therefore, delighted at the chance to dispose of some of his immense store of ivory in exchange for beads, cloth, guns and other novelties from Khartoum. Ibrahim left Bunyoro with 32,000 lbs. of ivory, worth about £9,630. He was not destined to get it to Khartoum without difficulty. In Madi country his 800 porters decamped overnight making it quite impossible for him to proceed. Baker did not trouble to conceal his delight at the Turk's predicament.

By the time the discoverer of Lake Albert returned to the Sudan the situation was changing. The Khedive was trying to tighten his grip on the area by appointing governors (mostly European) whose commission was to establish sound administration. They were also charged with stamping out the slave trade, which Ismail had promised Europe that he would eradicate. But while, with his usual suave charm, the Khedive was assuring foreign diplomats that everything was being done to expunge the curse of slave dealing from his dominions he was also selling ivory trade monopolies to the heads of the great Khartoum-based houses. And where white ivory was there black ivory was found also. There were other complications for the officials on the spot: they were expected to finance their administration out of ivory trading. This, it was urged, would provide them with ample funds to rule and would also enable them to foster legitimate trade. The real situation was very different as Baker discovered when he called at Khartoum before taking up his post in Equatoria:

'It was clearly contrary to all ideas of equity that the Government should purchase ivory in a country that had been leased to the traders. I was, therefore, compelled to investigate the matter with the assistance of Djiaffer Pasha, who had made the contract in the name of the Government. It was then explained that the *entire White Nile* was rented to the traders. The Government has assumed the right and monopoly of the river and, in fact, of any part of Africa that could be reached, south of Khartoum; thus no trader was permitted to establish himself, or even to start from Khartoum for the interior until he should have obtained a lease from the Government. If Central Africa had been already annexed, and the Egyptian Government had been established throughout the country, I should not have complained; but I now found my mission from the Khedive placed me within "a house divided against itself". I was to annex a country that was already leased out by the Government. My task was to suppress the slave trade, when the Khartoum authorities well knew that their tenants were slave-hunters; to establish legitimate commerce where the monopoly of trade had already been leased to traders; and to build up a government upon sound and just principles, that must of necessity ruin the slave-hunting and ivory-collecting parties of Khartoum.'

With the help of the governor of Khartoum, Baker and Sheikh Akad, the head of the firm with the Equatoria ivory concession, reached a compromise. Akad was to enjoy his monopoly for a further eighteen months, paying part of the rent in ivory. Thereafter Baker would be free to establish a government monopoly. The arrangement seemed perfectly reasonable in the civilised atmosphere of Khartoum: in the hostile world of the southern Sudan it was virtually impossible to enforce. The Akad representative was Abu Saud, one of the most notorious slavers ever to hit Africa. He commanded larger forces than the governor. Most of the more powerful chiefs were in league with him. Many of Baker's own station commanders were in Abu Saud's pay. The slaver intrigued against Baker and placed every obstacle in his way, while obsequiously avowing his loyalty to the Khedive and the Governor whenever he met the white man. The culmination of Abu Saud's treachery came in 1873 when he incited Kabarega, the ruler of Bunyoro, to murder the Governor and his men at Masindi, the capital of Bunyoro. The unfortunate Kabarega tried to comply. He first sent a supply of drugged native beer into Baker's stockade, planning to attack in force at night and overthrow the immobilised garrison. But the Bakers defeated him with tartaric acid, mustard and brine. Dosed with these powerful emetics, the stricken men survived the poison and were able to turn the tables on Kabarega.

Before this incident Baker had begun trading relations with the Banyoro. He had brought with him a variety of tempting goods which, he hoped, the people would be only too eager to receive in exchange for ivory:

'There were tin plates as bright as mirrors, crockery of various kinds, glasses, knives of many varieties, beautiful Manchester manufactures, such as Indian scarves, handkerchiefs, piece-goods, light-blue serge, chintzes, scarlet and blue blankets, blue and crimson cotton cloth, small mirrors, scissors, razors, watches, clocks, tin whistles, triangles, tambourines, toys, including small tin steamers, boats, carriages, Japanese spinning-tops, horn snakes, pop-guns, spherical quicksilvered globes, together with assortments of beads of many varieties.'

Thus did this self-assured child of the Industrial Revolution set about creating in the middle of Africa a demand for consumer durables—and all for ivory.

The prospects for replacing slave dealing with legitimate trade seemed good. Kabarega's storehouses were even more full of ivory than his father's had been, as tribute poured in from subsidiary chiefs and found no outlet:

'In Bunyoro an established value for a healthy young girl was that she was equal to a single elephant's tusk or a new shirt. A girl might be purchased in Uganda for thirteen English needles . . . In some cases we purchased ivory at 2,000% profit and both sellers and buyers felt perfectly contented. Here was free trade thoroughly established, the future was tinged with a golden hue. Ivory would be almost inexhaustible, as it would flow from both east and west to the market where such luxuries as two-penny handkerchiefs, ear-rings at a penny a pair, finger signet-rings at a shilling a dozen, could be obtained for such comparatively useless lumber as elephant tusks.'

And what of Abu Saud? The date for his departure had long passed but he was in no hurry to bring his commercial activities to an end. After the failure of his plot to slaughter the Governor's garrison, however, discretion overcame him. He retreated rapidly to Khartoum and then Cairo—doubtless to impress on the Government before Baker returned his own version of events in the Sudan. On his journey down river at the end of his tour in 1873 Baker took the first opportunity of telegraphing Cairo to advise the arrest of Abu Saud. The slaver was immediately seized and Baker had the satisfaction of seeing his arch enemy behind bars when he passed through Cairo. But a few months later fresh news of the notorious slaver reached Baker in England: he had been released from jail and appointed assistant to the new Governor of Equatoria!

Baker's successor was another famous Englishman, Charles Gordon. He governed Equatoria from 1874 to 1879 during which time the Khedive's avowed plans for the region began to be realised. Gordon successfully established a government monopoly in ivory. He could soon report: 'I am quite independent of the Khedive for money. In a year he had £48,000 from the province and I have spent say £20,000 at the outside, and have £60,000 worth of ivory here.' The activities of the Khartoumers were now severely restricted. One result of Gordon's ban on free trade was the forcing of Bunyoro to find a southern outlet for ivory. The appetite of the king and people for European trinkets had been whetted but Kabarega resisted Gordon's attempt to annexe his land and draw him into the Egyptian trade monopoly. Instead he succeeded in establishing contact with Zanzibari traders and a regular commercial relationship was set up with the dealers from south of the Lake.

In any case the days of the Sudanese ivory trade were numbered. In 1881, aroused by hatred of Egyptian imperialism and the many outrages committed in the northern Sudan by corrupt officials, Muhammad Ahmad, otherwise known as the Mahdi, raised the standard of revolt. Rapidly his fiery zeal burned through Kordofan, Darfur and Bahr el-Ghazal. Far to the south, in Equatoria, the Egyptian garrisons held out against the Mahdist advance under the leadership of the Governor, Dr Edouard Schnitzer—Emin Pasha—who had assumed command in Equatoria in 1879. A studious man with a keen sense of duty, he followed the example set by Gordon of doing everything possible for the development and improvement of the land and people under his control. He rid the country of the Khartoumers and put the administration on a sound footing. This involved the enthusiastic exploitation of the government ivory monopoly. Emin continued trading long after the Mahdist revolt had cut all his links with Europe and made it impossible to send ivory down the Nile. The ivory in the various government storehouses at Lado, Dufilé and Wadelai built up steadily until Emin had accumulated what must surely have been the largest ivory horde ever amassed by one man. It was this fact more than any other which ensured that he would not remain forever forgotten in the heart of Africa.

On 28th February 1885 a British relief force reached Khartoum only to discover that it had fallen to the Mahdi two days previously after a siege of 317 days. The world heard with horror of the massacre of 'Chinese' Gordon and his garrison. When news later reached Europe that there was in Equatoria another isolated white man stubbornly guarding the flag of civilisation against the encroaching forces of religious fanaticism and anarchy there was another outcry—there must not be another Khartoum tragedy. In 1887 there was a frenzy of concern to 'get Emin out'. Adventurers, government ministers, imperialists, newspaper editors, commercial speculators and a hundred and one interested parties campaigned for the organisation of expeditions to go to the relief of the beleaguered garrisons. Three such expeditions were eventually launched. Behind the humanitarian concerns of their leaders and backers lay the calculated possibilities of reimbursement from Emin's ivory stocks. The Governor of Equatoria received with mixed feelings the news of the plans being made on his behalf:

'You can imagine better than I can tell you that the heartfelt sympathy which has been expressed for me and my people in England . . . has richly repaid me for many of the sorrows and hardships I have undergone. . . . The work that Gordon paid for with his blood, I will strive to carry on, if not with his energy and genius, still according to his intentions and with his spirit. . . . All we would ask England to do is to bring about a better understanding with Uganda and to provide us with a free and safe way to the coast. This is all we want. Evacuate our territory? Certainly not!'

But Emin for all his undoubted sincerity and concern for his people, was a man of pliable gold and not steel. He lacked the military skill necessary to withstand the Mahdists and he was not the sort of man to stand up to the bullying of Henry Morton Stanley.

Stanley was the first 'rescuer' to reach Emin. The two men met on the banks of Lake Albert on 17th February 1889 after Stanley and his men had endured almost two years of the most appalling hardship in the foetid Congo forest. By then the explorer knew that it would be impossible to fetch out all Emin's ivory; his force was so depleted and the obstacles ahead so great that it would be hard enough to convey the Governor and his men to safety, without taking thousands of extra porters loaded with elephant tusks. This was very galling to Stanley who had just heard from A. J. Mounteney Jephson, the leader of the advanced party, the true extent of Emin's fabled ivory hoard:

'Before leaving the station (Wadelai), Kodi Aga took me round the storehouses and showed me the government ivory, of which there were vast quantities, all arranged in different heaps, according to the size of the tusks. There was one tusk showed me which weighed 140 lbs., and was the largest tusk I have ever seen in Africa. Emin told me also there were large stores of ivory in Dufilé, and he had somewhere about 1000 tusks in Monbuttu, which he had left in charge of one of the friendly chiefs of that country. The value of ivory in government storehouses, he said, was £75,000, but this was estimating it at the rate of 8s. a pound, but as the price of ivory is now 12s. a lb. at the coast, it would make the real value of the ivory in the Province £112,250.

'All this ivory would have to be abandoned, as we could never carry it down to the coast. It was grievous that so much money should have to be thrown away.

'The Pasha told me he had for three years given up collecting ivory, as he knew it would never be of any use to him; and had he continued to collect it, he would have had double the amount.'

On 10th April 1889 Emin Pasha abandoned his province and his ivory. His departure marked the ultimate failure to establish in the southern Sudan a stable administration based on legitimate trade in ivory. Anarchy and tribal warfare returned to the area and with them all the evils of unbridled slave and ivory trading. Peace and a degree of order were not restored for another ten years when the pretence of Egyptian *imperium* was replaced by the reality of British rule. For the relief of Emin Pasha was the prelude to the European colonial advance. In the following year Britain and Germany reached final agreement on their respective spheres of influence in East Africa. There followed months of diplomatic wrangles in London, Brussels, Rome and Paris about who had a claim to the upper Nile valley, from which Britain emerged brandishing a map on

which most of the disputed area was painted an encouraging
red. In 1898 she began to turn paper protectorates into practical
realities and set her seal on the title deeds of the Sudan in the
bloody battle of Omdurman. From the chaos created by rival
tribes, slavers, Egyptian governors and Mahdists a new pattern
was emerging.

That pattern was also emerging further south, in Tippu Tip's
old hunting grounds. Sometime in 1891 the 'King of the Congo'
had a conversation with A. J. Swann at Ujiji and what he said
was to prove prophetic in more ways than one:

' "I came here a young man," said Tippu Tip, "fought these
natives and subdued them, losing both friends and treasure
in the struggle. Is it not therefore mine by both your law
and ours?"

' "It is only yours so long as you use and govern it
properly."

' "Who is to be my judge?"

' "Europe!"

' "Aha! now you speak the truth. Do not let us talk of
justice; people are only just when it pays. The white man is
stronger than I am; they will eat my possessions as I ate those
of the pagans, and . . . *some one will eat up yours!*"

'Swann was not to be drawn by ominous prognostications.

' "Europe has sickened of your cruel slave operations," he
said, "and determined to stop them."

' "It seems to me that Europe is determined to ruin me. Is
that it?"

' "Yes, if you do not abandon your trade." '

Soon after this conversation Tippu Tip made his way eastwards to Zanzibar for the last time, there to live the rest of his
life in honoured peace and prosperity and to write his auto-
biography. As he made his final journey along the familiar trail
from Ujiji to Tabora and Bagamoyo he may well have reflected
upon the curious twists of fate he had seen in the previous
decade. The pioneer white missionaries and explorers of the
1870s had given way to well-equipped expeditions, government
agents and men who came to hunt 'his' elephants and frown
upon his trade. In 1885 the Germans had planted their flag at
the coast. At the same time the agents of the Congo Free State,

led by H. M. Stanley, were encroaching on his preserves from the west and diverting through their own territory the flow of ivory.

Tippu Tip's empire was caught between the jaws of a white vice and though the movement was very slow these jaws were perceptibly closing. Tippu Tip could see what was happening because he had always maintained close, even friendly, relations with all the Europeans he met. It was not so for many of Tippu Tip's subordinates and colleagues. In 1886 one of his agents, Bwana Nzige, organised a raid on the C.F.S. post at Stanley Falls. It was burned to the ground and its Belgian garrison slaughtered. This was a serious setback for the Free State which lacked the forces necessary to impose its will against determined opposition.

It was at this point that Henry Stanley, on behalf of the C.F.S., proposed a solution as simple as it was subtle. He met Tippu Tip at Zanzibar and proposed that the old slaver should return to his old haunts as Free State Governor of Stanley Falls. The arch-poacher was to be made a game keeper. The idea amused Tippu Tip enormously but its advantages to both sides were obvious: the Arabs could have one last fling in the magnificent ivory hunting grounds on the forest fringe and, by employing the one man capable of maintaining peace in the area, the Belgians would have time to strengthen their position. He agreed to accompany Stanley and the two men travelled round Africa by ship in order to ascend the Congo river from the west. As the steamer made its way up the great river which only a dozen years before Stanley had cautiously ventured down by canoe the Arab could see for himself the symbols of European progress—administrative posts, landing stages, trading steamers coming down laden with ivory. If he had entertained any doubts about the ultimate triumph of the white man they now vanished.

For over three years Tippu Tip maintained peace with difficulty at Stanley Falls. He accumulated another vast stock of ivory and despatched it eastwards, determined to make as much profit as possible from his last trading venture. He encouraged his fellow Zanzibaris to do the same but they could not share his view of the inevitable. Even Rumaliza, his right hand man, was unable to see the difference between the C.F.S.

agents and the missionaries and explorers of an earlier age. He later explained his point of view to Swann:

'You and the other Europeans, arrived here (Ujiji) with proper introductions from the coast, which we always respected, and never caused you trouble of any kind. These Belgian officers came, and the first thing we hear about this is that they are attacking our outposts and claiming the whole country. Not one has visited us, or sent his flag, or had the courtesty to approach us in any way. . . . We received information that they were occupying the road between here and our trading centres, and had stopped all traffic in ivory. Our head-men sent asking for instructions, and we told them to defend our trade, but not to attack the white men unless fired on by their troops.

'. . . We cannot have people running about the country with armed men attacking our soldiers, and, as they did not think it necessary to acknowledge our presence, we on our part declined to put ourselves to the trouble of crossing the lake to superintend the operations of our half-wild followers. The Belgians have themselves to thank for all this trouble.'

The time for such petulance and self-righteousness was past.

When Tippu Tip set out from Stanley Falls at the end of 1890 he left his son, Sef, behind with instructions to convey the rest of his ivory to the coast. He never saw his son or his ivory again. In 1892 the main Arab centres in the Congo rose against the Belgians. East of the lake the Germans were advancing. When they hoisted their flag at Ujiji Rumaliza personally hauled it down and trampled it into the dust. Then he fled to join his colleagues. While the Germans possessed themselves of the Arab's large ivory stocks at Ujiji and Tabora, Rumaliza and his followers fought and lost a series of battles against the Belgians. The last conflict took place on the banks of the River Luama in October 1893. After several hours of savage fighting Rumaliza disappeared into the forest with only four companions. All along the river bank the bodies of Arabs and Belgians lay on the churned mud. Somewhere among them lay the shattered remains of Sef bin Hamed el Muriebi.

6

'Khiva, the Zulu boy, saw his master fall, and, brave lad as he was, turned and flung his assegai straight into the elephant's face. It stuck in his trunk.
'With a scream of pain, the brute siezed the poor Zulu, hurled him to the earth, and placing one huge foot on to his body about the middle, twined its trunk about his upper part and tore him in two.
'We rushed up mad with horror, and fired again and again, till presently the elephant fell upon the fragments of the Zulu.'

—Rider Haggard, KING SOLOMON'S MINES

Take-over Bid

By 1890 almost the whole of Africa had been divided up between the leading powers of Europe but it took many years for the African 'Raj' to become a reality. Military posts, administrative centres, roads and railways had to be built. New patterns of law and order had to be established. New concepts of civilisation had to be imposed. Ways had to be found to make the colonies self-sufficient. In short, a wild continent had to be tamed, and while all this was going on the white ivory hunters had a field day.

All this activity awakened among European men and women a greater interest in the Dark Continent. There was an enormous demand for books and magazine articles about Africa. Officials and sportsmen, however long or short their stay in the new colonies, wrote up their adventures for popular consumption. Novelists and serial-writers like Rider Haggard created for the common taste a new, mystical, romantic 'Africa'—a land whose innumerable terrors included man-eating lions, poisonous snakes and spiders, 'voodoo' rites and cannibals; a land in the heart of whose impenetrable jungle lay lost cities, forgotten tribes, undiscovered mines of gold and diamonds, and fabulous 'elephants' graveyards' where thousands of tusks lay waiting for the intrepid explorer.

Paradoxically, at the same time as this romantic myth was

being propagated the real romance of Africa, as far as the hunter was concerned, was fast disappearing. Sir Harry Johnston, in his foreword to A. J. Swann's *Fighting the Slave Hunters in Central Africa* wrote:

'The Africa of Mr Swann's days, with its unlimited and even dangerous wild beasts, its men and women just emerging from the Age of Stone, The *Nyika* innocent of eucalyptus groves, dense forests scarcely altered since the Miocene, Man at his most barbarous and most heroic, has disappeared in favour of railways, motors, telegraph, negroes that are drilled in European fashion, prosperous mission-schools and technical institutes, the bang, bang, bang of the slaughtering British sportsmen, the lisping accents of the lady traveller who is trying to write a book about Africa in a four-months' tour (lapped in luxury as she passes from one hospital station to another), the Africa of the cinematograph and the gramophone record, of fashionable diplomacy, highly-trained administrators, royal guests, and banished malaria.'

Johnston was writing in 1910.

This was the situation over much of tropical Africa by the turn of the century and white hunters with the pioneer spirit were seeking their fortunes in the slowly diminishing area beyond the limits of effective colonial rule. But in the transition period, 1880–1900, the sportsman still enjoyed a freedom limited only by the supply of elephant and the extent of his own stamina. South Africa was, by this time, largely destocked and hunters from the south concentrated their activities on the land between the Limpopo and the Zambezi. Others entered the continent from the west or east to challenge the Arab monopoly in what is now Zaire. The last 'sporting thrust' into Africa was into Kenya and Uganda in the 1880s and 1890s. This eventually linked up with the southward thrust into the Sudan and Bunyoro.

One great sporting life links the pioneering days of South and East Africa. Frederick Courtenay Selous landed at Algoa Bay in 1871. He was 19 years old—he had £400 in his pocket, and his head was full of the sporting adventures he had read about in the works of Baldwin and Gordon Cumming. He worked his way slowly inland but not until he reached Matabeleland, 1,400 miles away from the Cape, did he encounter elephant. His first attempt to bag a tusker revealed his inexperience and the inadequacy of his weapon: Selous and his colleague approached to within thirty yards of a group of seven bulls 'and fired simultaneously; he at one standing broadside, and I at another facing me. Our Hottentot boy also fired, and, as the animals turned, a volley was given by our Kaffirs, about ten of whom carried guns. Not an elephant, however, seemed any the worse.' Selous followed the animals and once more positioned himself for a telling shot. Unfortunately his bearer, in his excitement, had overcharged Selous' gun. There was an enormous explosion; the hunter went one way and his weapon went the other. As if that were not sufficient misfortune, one of his African servants was shot dead during the battle by an excited and over-zealous colleague. The party eventually made a good haul of ivory but Selous' right arm was very badly sprained and it was ten days before he regained full use of it.

The young hunter rapidly learned the lessons of such early misfortunes. He marched on to the Zambezi, gaining many fine game specimens and sufficient ivory to pay for his hunting. But living by the gun was a financially precarious business. He relied more and more on the visits of wealthy sportsmen for whom he acted as guide. When, as in 1884, such an arrangement fell through Selous could find himself in difficulties. 'I am very sorry indeed, for being with Jameson, who is, of course, a rich man, I should have been free from the constant anxiety which now overhangs me like a black cloud as to whether I shall be able to pay my debts. It is so very easy to lose a hundred pounds in live stock, from sickness, drought, hunger, etc., and so hard, so very hard, to make it.'

Matabeleland and Mashonaland (roughly conterminous with modern Rhodesia) were Selous' principal haunts until 1893. There was game to be found here which had long disappeared further south. But even here the situation was changing rapidly. On his later expedition Selous ventured deep into the land beyond the Zambezi. Between 1890 and 1893 much of his energy was devoted to urging and practically supporting the British South Africa Company's annexation of Rhodesia. Selous knew the country better than any other white man; he knew and profoundly disliked the Ndebele chief Lobengula; he knew and disliked almost as much the Portuguese colonial officials who also wished to annexe the area. With this knowledge he concluded that British rule was the only hope for the security and peace of Matabeleland and Mashonaland. He pressed Rhodes to send his agents into the area and when the British South Africa Company's pioneer column advanced in June-September 1890, Selous went on ahead to cut a road to Mashonaland. To him also fell the task of negotiating mining concessions with the Shona chiefs. Faced with the *fait accompli* of colonial advance, Selous, like many other sportsmen, actively supported the claims of his own country. Though he had chosen the solitary life and had cut himself off from white civilisation he remained a patriot. Much good did it do him: he received no recognition of his services from the British government, and Cecil Rhodes, who openly acknowledged Selous as 'the man above all others to whom we owe Rhodesia to the British Crown', discarded the great hunter as soon as he had no further use for him.

Selous returned to England at the end of 1892 and soon afterwards became engaged to be married. But even his prospective bride had to take second place to Africa in the hunter's affections. Selous was back in Rhodesia within months when the Ndebele war of 1893 broke out and returned again in 1896 to help combat the Ndebele and Shona risings (the last concerted rebellion against imperial rule).

By this time Selous' exploits and writings had made him one of the most celebrated sportsmen of the age. His services were sought as speaker and adviser on African subjects. He helped ex-President Theodore Roosevelt of the U.S.A. to organise hunting expeditions to East Africa. It was to this part of the continent that Selous' hunting instincts now drew him. He made three safaris in British East Africa in the early years of the new century and recognised it as one of the few remaining areas prolific in big game. His main objective on these expeditions was to complete his collection of sporting trophies. Now that his reputation and income were assured he hunted for pleasure and scientific interest only. East Africa's ivory was of little interest to him. But East Africa itself had got its hooks into him, as it has into so many ex-patriates. He confided to a friend in 1912, '. . . what I dislike more than anything else in English life is the crowds of people everywhere . . . I am already longing to be in Africa again. If only Mrs Selous would be happy there, I would rather live in East Africa than in this country.'

Frederick Selous did not return as a settler to East Africa but he did die there, which is what he would have wished. On the outbreak of the First World War he pestered the War Office for permission to take part in the East African campaign, despite the fact that he was 65 years old. His tenacity eventually wore down official opposition and Selous sailed again for his beloved Africa. He was killed in a skirmish with German forces near the Rufiji River (in what is now southern Tanzania) on 4th January 1917 and was buried on the plain at the heart of what later became a wildlife sanctuary—the Selous Game Reserve.

The area between the Zambezi and Kenya which Selous did not venture into was the area which had for several decades been the preserve of Arab and African ivory hunters. The effects of their activities were appallingly obvious to European visitors like Joseph Thomson, who led a Royal Geographical Society expedition to the Great Lakes in 1879–80:

'People talk as if the ivory of Africa were inexhaustible. It is commonly supposed that, if European traders could but establish themselves in the interior, fortunes could be made. Nothing could be more absurd. Let me simply mention a fact. In my sojourn of fourteen months, during which I passed over an immense area of the Great Lakes region, *I never once saw a single elephant.* Twenty years ago they roamed over those countries unmolested, and now they have been almost utterly exterminated. Less than ten years ago Livingstone spoke about the abundance of elephants at the south end of Tanganyika—how they came about his camp or entered the villages with impunity. Not one is now to be found. The ruthless work of destruction has gone on with frightful rapidity.'

Indiscriminate slaughter and the retreat of surviving herds into less accessible places seem to be the inevitable results of the passion for ivory. The colonial governments which took over the greater part of Africa between 1884 and 1900 were well aware of this but in practice there was an inconsistency in their approach to the problem. This inconsistency sprang from two conflicting principles: the colonial governors were responsible for the preservation of natural resources; they also had to make the colonies pay. Throughout East and Central Africa the only valuable export which could be exploited in the short term was ivory. When the plans for a railway in British East Africa were under discussion it was suggested that the government could rely on at least 120 tons of ivory per annum being despatched to the coast at a haulage of £45 per ton. Ivory obtained by private individuals and commercial concerns would, of course, be subject to customs duty. These were attractive arguments and for a few years sportsmen were encouraged to make forays into the new colonial territories. But soon the need for regulations was recognised. German East Africa brought in game laws in 1896 which obliged hunters to be licensed and prohibited the killing of cows and immature elephants. Two years later the Germans went a stage further, restricting hunting rights to a small group of professional elephant hunters who were forced to give to the government one tusk from every pair taken. In 1897 the British followed suit with similar regulations and the demarcation of the first reserves.

The first sportsmen to penetrate what is now Kenya found the virgin hunting grounds as rich as the Cape, Matabeleland and the eastern Congo had once been. Joseph Thomson, who had spoken so disparagingly of the prospects for ivory hunters further south, was astonished at the elephant population of the Mount Kenya–Rift Valley region when he journeyed there in 1883–4. He saw tusks lying rotting on the ground and reported, 'a tusk of ivory worth £150 in England can either be picked up or bought for a shilling's worth of beads.' Count Samuel Teleki von Szek and his companion Lieutenant Ludwig von Hohnel were the first white men to reach Lake Rudolf in northern Kenya (1887) and they were overwhelmed by the abundant wild life of the area. It was, they believed, the richest region for ivory in all Africa. They returned home with a handsome profit as well as well-deserved reputations as explorers.

Hunters flocked to British and German East Africa to cash in on what was probably the last opportunity to make a fortune from ivory. A few succeeded and were very little embarrassed by the game laws introduced in the 1890s. In 1899 Sir Harry

Johnston, Commissioner for Uganda, complained to the Prime Minister Lord Salisbury:

'Even in regard to persons supposed to be sportsmen pure and simple, who come out to this part of the world to shoot big game, I would point out to your Lordship that behind their profession of sport there is often a very practical purpose lurking. Lord Delamere, for instance, left this part of the country last year with £14,000 worth of ivory (as declared in the custom house at Eldama Ravine), his medical officer (Dr Atkinson) who remained behind, has been steadily shooting elephants ever since, apparently without much regard for the provisions of the Uganda Game Regulations.'

If a line can be drawn between a genuine sportsman and a mere exploiter of the brute creation it is a very fine one. There is no doubt which side of it Arthur Neumann, one of the East African pioneers, stands on. 'I look upon him as the last of the real genuine hunters of African big game.' This was Selous' opinion of him and it was shared by many others who could claim to be experts. Neumann was Selous' exact contemporary; born in 1850 he arrived in Natal at the age of 18 and did his early hunting in South Africa. It was not until 1893 that he arrived at Mombasa to lead his first safari into British East Africa. In the next few years he became a living legend and is still regarded by many as the greatest of all elephant hunters.

Like every good sportsman Neumann was a keen observer and lover of nature. Between 1894 and 1896, for instance, he made the first collection and catalogue of East African butterflies (170 species). There was in him a self-confessed cruel streak: in his books and articles he described with minute detail and even relish the deaths of some of his victims. However, he also described with equal candour his own near-fatal experience. This occurred when he came face to face with an angry cow elephant on a forest path:

'I could also see that there was a large calf following her as she came. I stood to face her and threw up my rifle to fire at her head as she came on, at a quick run, without raising her trunk or uttering a sound, realising in a moment that this was the only thing to do, so short was the distance separating us. The click of the striker was the only result of pulling the trigger. No cartridge had entered the barrel on my working the bolt after the last shot, though the empty case had flown out! In this desperate situation I saw at once that my case was well-nigh hopeless. The enraged elephant was by this time within a few strides of me; the narrow path was walled in on each side with thick scrub. To turn and run down the path in an instinctive effort to escape was all I could do, the elephant overhauling me at every step. As I ran those few yards I made one spasmodic attempt to work the mechanism of the treacherous magazine, and, pointing the muzzle behind me without looking round, tried it again; but it was no go. She was now all but upon me. Dropping the gun, I sprang out of the path to the right and threw myself down among some brushwood in the vain hope that she might pass on. But she was too close; and, turning with me like a terrier after a rabbit, she was on top of me as soon as I was down. In falling I had turned over onto my back, and lay with my feet towards the path, face upwards, my head being propped up by brushwood. Kneeling over me (but fortunately not touching me with her legs, which must, I suppose, have been on each side of mine), she made three distinct lunges at me, sending her left tusk through the biceps of my right arm and stabbing me between the right ribs, at the same time pounding my chest with her head (or rather, I suppose, the thick part of her trunk between the tusks) and crushing in my ribs on the same side. At the first butt some part of her head came in contact with my face, barking my nose and taking patches of skin off other spots, and I thought my head would be crushed, but it slipped back and was not touched again. I was wondering at the time how she would kill me; for of course I never thought anything but that the end of my hunting was come at last. What hurt me was the grinding my chest underwent. Whether she supposed she had killed me, or whether it was that she disliked the smell of my blood, or bethought her of her calf, I cannot tell; but she then left me and went her way.'

Neumann was incredibly lucky not to have been trampled to death or to have had a lung pierced. He was even luckier in the devotion and attentiveness of his African servants. Nothing illustrates more dramatically how dependent white hunters were on their African companions than the story of how Arthur Neumann was nursed back to health. His bearers bathed his wounds, rigged a makeshift stretcher and carried his bleeding body in careful relays back to the base camp where bandages were available to dress his wounds.

For three months Neumann was virtually a complete invalid, a mass of torn muscles, broken bones and suppurating sores. Pain, sleeplessness, bouts of malaria and dysentery made him a difficult and ill-tempered patient. His party's food supply gradually dwindled, and Neumann was quite unable to fulfill his role of meat provider. At any time the hunter's companions could have deserted him and gone off with his guns, ivory and trade goods. Instead they stayed to cope with his distressing symptoms, to minister to his needs, to endure his tantrums and to nurse him slowly back to health. Such faithfulness provides a valuable counter balance to the complaints made by other hunters about the greed, laziness, cowardice and stupidity of the 'natives'.

All the great ivory hunters found the cheerful camaraderie they enjoyed with their African servants to be one of the most appealing aspects of life on safari. Indeed, as a rule of thumb, one can form a fairly accurate assessment of a hunter from his attitude towards his black companions.

If one did not know, for example, that William Cotton Oswell was one of the sporting giants of all time one might go far towards deducing it from his tribute to his servant John Thomas:

'. . . he was a perfect servant to a very imperfect master, who, now that his friend is dead, feels that he did not value him half enough, though he never loved man better . . . [it was little] matter to us whether our brother was black or white. . . . As a grand specimen of manhood, good nature, faithfulness and cheerful endurance, I never met his equal, white or black.'

As trackers the Africans were priceless. A skilled guide could not only follow an elephant some miles distant, but, from tracks, droppings, broken branches, disturbed insect and animal life, could discern its size, sex and how far ahead it was. C. H.

Stigand used three trackers in Nyasaland whose talents inter-locked perfectly:

'For the first hour or so Ulaya used to fly away with the track; he was practically never at fault and not a sign escaped him. If after that time the track was still old, he generally used to sit down and say it was no good, and nothing would induce him to take any further trouble over it. Chimalambe then took up the spooring and for hour after hour he would slowly and painfully worry it out, making frequent mistakes, losing the track and returning to pick it up again, but he was prepared to go on in the same way all day . . . Matola was the brave member of the trio who invariably took the lead when the trail was fresh and dangerous animals were close at hand.'

This same Matola proved his worth on one occasion when Stigand found himself in a tight corner. The hunter had wounded a young bull elephant and now found himself uncom-fortably close to the enraged animal with an empty gun in his hands:

'. . . the rifle was taken out of my hands and I found Matola, who had counted the shots, serving me the second rifle as a waiter might offer a dish. By some oversight it had not been loaded, and I had given strict orders that none of my men were ever to load or unload my rifles. Being a good soldier, Matola had not disobeyed this order, even under these extreme circumstances, but had gone the nearest to loading it he could. The breach was open, and he was holding the clip in position with his thumb just over the magazine. All I had to do was to press it down, as I took hold of the rifle, close the bolt, and I was ready to fire.'

Such stories abound in the writings of the hunters. A sports-man who chose his men with care and looked after them well could be fairly sure of faithful and good-natured service in return. The camps were cheerful, bustling places: the porters argued over who should carry the lighter loads; bearers and trackers disputed as to who had taken the greatest part in some

recent exploit; and always there was singing—usually im-
promtu songs about the events of the day's march.

But to return to Arthur Neumann. His near fatal encounter
with the elephant in 1895 in no measure dampened his ardour
for the sport. He made a further three expeditions to East
Africa in the next ten years most of which time was spent in
what is now northern Kenya, an area almost unvisited by white
men. He found an abundance of elephant throughout the area
between Mount Kenya and Lake Rudolph (much of which is
now within the boundaries of the Samburu Game Reserve). On
his last journey (1905–6) he brought to the coast ivory worth
£4,500. By this time strict game laws were in operation. In all
probability the figure of £4,500 represents only a fraction of his
profit on earlier trips. This can scarcely have involved the
killing of less than 200–250 elephant. Neumann encountered
and disposed of some of the finest specimens of bush elephant
ever seen. Many of them were over ten feet six inches in height
at the shoulder and carried enormous tusks. Neumann's
personal best was a tusk of 116 lb. His haul was not, of course,
made up of such monumental pieces of ivory; cow tusks (he
was not squeamish about shooting cows if nothing better
presented itself) seldom weighed more than 24 lb. each.

A successful expedition brought its own problems. A hunter
finding himself in country teeming with elephant was often
faced with a dilemma: should he stay where he was and amass
as large a horde of ivory as possible, knowing that he would have
difficulty transporting it back to the coast, or should he stop
as soon as he had enough tusks for his party to cope with? Most
of the carrying was done by human porters as the many tse-tse
areas made it difficult to use pack animals over long distances
and the best porters could only be hired at the coast, at the
beginning of an expedition (the Nyamwezi who were among the
first great ivory traders of East Africa were still reckoned to be
the best porters). It was hardly feasible for a hunter to employ
an army of carriers in the hope that his luck would be excep-
tionally good. It therefore happened quite often that a sportsman found himself three or four hundred miles inland with more
ivory than his men could handle. He then had two choices: he
could bury part of his cache and return for it later, hoping
against hope to find it intact; or he could haggle with local

chiefs over the hire of extra porters. If he took the latter course he usually found himself on the wrong end of the bargain, paying through the nose for inferior porters. On one occasion C. H. Stigand experienced such an *embarras de richesse* and hit upon the scheme of disguising his buried horde. He surmounted the obvious freshly dug mound with a wooden cross, hoping that passing white men would take it for a hunter's grave while Africans would regard it as 'medicine' (i.e. a magic fetish). His ruse worked for, though rain exposed the topmost tusks the cache remained untouched until Stigand was able to collect it.

The end of a safari was a memorable occasion as Neumann records:

'At last, on 1st October, we once more entered Mombasa; and the men—decked in showy clothes, and headed by drummers hammering out, in perfect time, the regular "safari" beat—enjoyed the long-looked-forward-to parade through the streets. And a picturesque sight it is to see a string of porters, with gleaming ivory arcs on their shoulders, threading slowly the narrow streets, thronged with dusky but cleanly-clad onlookers; the leading men jumping up and dancing about with their hundredweight tusks, to show off before their admiring female friends. Indeed, it is often difficult to get them along at all, so proud and excited are they at entering their metropolis again after all the adventures of so long a journey.'

The activities of white hunters, as well as the continued slaughter of elephants by Africans and Arabs steadily and inevitably took their toll on the herds of East Africa. Had it not been for the introduction of game laws, which were beginning to 'bite' by about 1910, the elephant population would have disappeared as completely from this part of the continent as it did from others. Many contemporary observers tried to calculate the annual death toll of elephants based on ivory export figures but there were too many imponderables for accurate estimates to be made: What was the true average weight per tusk? What proportion of the ivory which reached the coast was taken from dead elephants or from long-hidden caches? Extant records show that 488,600 lb. of ivory passed through Zanzibar in 1859 and this was a fairly typical figure; exports rarely dropped below 400,000 lb. until the end of the century when Mombasa began to challenge Zanzibar's mercantile supremacy. Livingstone reckoned that 44,000 African elephants were slain in 1870 to meet the demands of the English market alone and Commander D. E. Blunt ventured the more precise figure 46,980 elephants per annum for the same trade. The estimate of the Gazette of Zanzibar and East Africa (5th December 1894) that 65,000 animals were killed annually throughout the continent is probably near the truth. Even the introduction of conservation laws did not make a dramatic impact on this figure, as Messrs Rowland Ward Ltd reported in 1914:

'. . . it seems probable that during the last few years the average sales of ivory in London, Liverpool, Antwerp, Lisbon and Germany have together amounted to not less than 2,500,000 lb. annually. The average weight of the tusks which go to make up this enormous total is certainly under 20 lb. But if it be taken at that figure, that would give 40 lb weight of ivory on the average, for each elephant killed on which basis 62,500 elephants would be required to supply the annual toll of 2,500,000 lb of ivory. Even if it can be shown that a considerable amount of this ivory has not come from freshly killed elephants, but has long been buried in native storehouses, and that in addition a small quantity of Asiatic ivory also came on the European market, it seems impossible to doubt that the minimum number of African elephants now annually slain must amount to at least 50,000.'

It is difficult to concede the writer's assertion that the majority of tusks were under 20 lb. in weight, particularly after the introduction of laws forbidding the killing of cows and immature elephants. Yet however we may quibble over details the proven carnage of these magnificent animals is horrific when we recall that the present elephant population of the entire continent is probably of the order of 300,000.

To what end was all this slaughter? Most of the markets for ivory were traditional ones of long standing. Some new uses were found for the substance in the nineteenth century and some new countries (notably the U.S.A.) joined the list of ivory importers, but most tusks still went to Bombay, Peking, London and Hamburg. There was no substitute for ivory as a medium for delicate carving and for a variety of more humdrum uses. Piano keys, billiard balls, handles for umbrellas and gentlemen's canes, paper knives, serviette-rings and false teeth—these were only a few of the myriad everyday uses found in the West for this semi-precious commodity. More exotic artefacts abounded to tickle the fancy of the European *nouveau riche*: miniature ornaments, statuettes and crucifixes from the cunning craftsmen of Dieppe, St Claude, Geislingen and Erbach; delicate fans and boudoir articles from Spain; inlaid butts for American six-shooters; applied ornament on furniture, guitars, piano accordions and a variety of other musical instruments. Toys, buttons, chess pieces, riding-whips—there seemed to be few uses to which this beautiful, hard-wearing and easily-worked substance could not be put. Nor was it only the solid ivory which was valuable. The cuttings and shavings from ivory workshops were carefully gathered and sacked to be sent on to yet other manufactories making Indian ink, jewellers' polish and fertiliser. It was even made into ivory jelly to amuse the novelty-seeking palates of the wealthy.

But it was still the Orient which remained the principal importer of ivory. No European craftsman could equal the incredible skill of Indian, Chinese and Japanese carvers. Expressive netsuke, lace-like panels for jewel caskets, dragons, buddhas and those astonishing concentric, perforated spheres, moving freely, one inside another—it was the makers of such masterpieces as these who fully exploited the possibilities of the medium. Much eastern manufacture was for export but ivory continued to be important as a status symbol of wealth and rank within oriental society. Craftsmen were kept well employed producing bangles, bracelets, personal ornaments, inlaid royal thrones and amusing trinkets. Demand always exceeded supply. Few figures are available but it is known that 6,000 tusks per year entered British India through the port of Bombay alone.

The ponderous advance of colonial administration into the interior drove before it an extraordinary human agglomeration. Slavers, fugitives from justice, white hunters, brigands, all those who had no cause to welcome the coming of efficient government, were pushed together into the wilder parts of the continent. In the year that Edward VII died Henry Darley found himself amidst very strange companions in the untamed land of the Ethiopia-Kenya-Uganda border. Somali, Ethiopian and Arab freebooters thronged the area collecting all the ivory and slaves they could and trying to keep at bay the agents of British and Ethiopian imperialism. At Maji, 125 miles north of Lake Rudolf, Darley fell in with the Shangalla chief Serie, a powerful ruler who commanded 3,000 guns. Serie made him an incredible offer: why not join forces and hold the area together? In return for the white man's support the Shangalla chief promised to fill Darley's hut to the roof with ivory. Darley is candid about his response: 'I had to decline the offer, much as I would have liked to have thrown in my lot with him, chiefly because I saw no way of ever leaving the country with my spoils.' Small wonder that the Englishman should have regarded the local rulers as 'the best of fellows'.

In fact these dusky idols with their merciless raids on the defenceless, their treachery to their titular overlords and their perpetual feuds had turned a vast area of the Ethiopian foothills into a wasteland. When Darley reached Mandara further north (near Jima) he saw for himself the full extent of the slave trade. He observed one caravan comprising, in his estimation, over 12,000 captives, take four days to pass through the town:

'I can lay no claim to being a philanthropist, far from it, but I can say with truth that I have never seen a more heart-rending sight . . . It was worse than war . . . after the last had gone by I saw an old woman supporting herself with a stick, hobbling after them.

'I said to her in Amharic; "Where are you going to, mother? Do you want the Abyssinians to catch you?"

'She answered, "What do I care? They have killed my husband and carried off all my children and grandchildren. I have no home left, so I follow them to wherever they go." '

Amidst all the chaos at Maji, Darley had to offer his protection to British subjects in the area. Most of them were Sudanese, Swahili or Baluchi traders and the worst scoundrels imaginable but had he not given way to their clamourings for sanctuary and even, in some cases, paid their debts, they and their goods would have been seized by Serie. It was ironical that Darley who had no love for the commercial riff-raff and scarcely more for the British official class should have found himself an acting, unpaid district officer. It was that word 'unpaid' which rankled with him most:

'. . . money, time, trouble, even life, spent in the altruistic endeavour to assist the British Government must of necessity be its own reward to the private individual. The British official mind hates to be disturbed in the even tenor of its way, its point of view being, "Why does this confounded fellow interfere! It is no business of his." As for the money spent, repayment is out of the question, for, in Africa, from the greatest governor, to the last joined policeman, all will answer any suggestion to that effect, by the words, "There is no fund out of which you can be repaid".'

Despite the fact that Darley was among those who made a small fortune from ivory hunting beyond the bounds of effective British jurisdiction (he frequently bagged tusks of 90 lb. and over in northern Kenya) he was very bitter about those 'closed areas' which were only red on the map:

'The shades of the many Britishers whom the Abyssinians and their allies have murdered are still waiting for [punitive] expeditions, as also are the thousands of British subjects under the so-called British Protectorate, who have been killed or carried off into slavery by the Abyssinians . . .
'The poor natives, martyrs to British "protection", . . . Their country is a "closed district", closed to anybody who might expose the ineffectiveness of their regime, but wide open to murderers, robbers, slave raiders, or any ruffian who likes to take his chance there.'

Many of the professional hunters who worked in Africa during the twilight of the great sporting era had this mixed, almost hypocritical, attitude towards the spread of colonial control. But however this handful of adventurers felt about it, the inexorable advance of officialdom was proceeding and erecting carefully its barriers of red tape. Yet, for the remaining great hunters there was to be one last spree of unrestricted elephant shooting—in the Lado Enclave.

7

*'All sorts of men came. Government employees threw up their jobs.
Masons, contractors, marine engineers, army men, hotel keepers and
others came, attracted by tales of fabulous quantities of ivory . . . It
might almost have been a gold rush.'*

—W. D. M. Bell, WANDERINGS OF AN ELEPHANT HUNTER

Hunter's Paradise

John Boyes called himself the 'King of the Kikuyu'. He had
established his base in the 'closed area' of the Kenya Highlands
in 1898, in complete disregard of official prohibition. By im-
pressing the people with his guns and other curiosities he had
gained a reputation among several clans as a powerful medicine
man and before long he was able to organise bands of Kikuyu
warriors for elephant hunting expeditions and quickly built up
an impressive store of ivory. For two and a half years Boyes
'lived native', systematically shooting and buying all the ivory
he could lay hands on. He was able to buy ivory on extremely
favourable terms, his market not having been spoiled by other
foreign traders. Unlike other hunters he worked from an
established base and became intimately involved with the life
of the people. He led military expeditions against rival communities, he advised the Kikuyu elders on agricultural methods
and provided medicines for the sick.

The inevitable day at last dawned when the British authorities
felt able to extend their power over Kikuyuland. A khaki-clad
detachment arrived one morning; Boyes and the local chiefs
were summoned to appear before the representative of the
imperial presence. The 'King of Kikuyu' was not well received
by his fellow Englishmen. They took exception to his men being
in 'uniform' (Boyes had devised a simple livery for his followers)
and wearing badges of rank. 'My chief offence, however, was the
fact that I was flying the Union Jack, which my men carried

with them, as they were accustomed to do on all their expeditions . . . it seemed that it was a most serious offence for an Englishman to display the flag under which he had been born and for which he had fought, unless he had some position in the official oligarchy of the country.'

Boyes was used to the hostility between colonial authorities and independent white men but even so he was taken completely aback by the next move of the officials. They arrested him and despatched him to Mombasa to face trial for having 'waged war, set shauries (organised meetings with African leaders), personated Government, [undertaken] six punitive expeditions and committed dacoity' (this last colourful Indian expression meaning brigandage was presumably employed by some pompous official because it sounded impressive). British justice proved kinder to Boyes than British law enforcement agents; he was acquitted without a stain on his character. More than that, he was sent back to Kikuyuland as a government intelligence agent.

But John Boyes was too restless a spirit to be tied to official procedures and routines. Before many months passed he was off in search of further adventures in Ethiopia. That expedition over, he returned to Mount Kenya. He was there on 17 December 1909 when in Brussels Leopold II, King of the Belgians, died. When the news reached him John Boyes packed his bags and headed for the Lado Enclave. He was one of many; as the wind of rumour carried the news of Leopold's death from village to village, camp to camp, every fortune-seeker in East Africa and beyond hurriedly prepared for a safari to the Sudan-Free State border. The Lado Enclave was open!

The Lado Enclave—the very words have an alluring, mysterious ring about them. A large wedge of savannah between the Congo Forest and the Nile, it had for years been a refuge for Africans fleeing from slavers, of slavers fleeing from justice and of elephant herds fleeing from ivory hunters. This was the corner of Equatoria which Emin Pasha had held out tenaciously against the Mahdists and from which he had been so reluctantly rescued by Stanley. A thousand miles from the nearest coastline, the Enclave had been virtually inaccessible to foreigners. This did not prevent the imperial map makers quarrelling over the area in the 1890s, after the collapse of the Mahdist state.

In 1894 Britain claimed all the territory bordering the upper Nile but gave to Leopold's Free State a lease on the area to the west of the river. This vague tract of territory was limited by the French to an area bounded by the 30°E and 5°30'N lines of longitude and latitude. The lease was to expire six months after King Leopold's death.

When that singularly unpleasant monarch breathed his last in December 1909 the Congo Free State agents in the unhealthy Lado Enclave did not wait a further six months before they withdrew. They beat a hasty westward retreat to the more congenial stations along the Congo. Britain had no jurisdiction over the area until June 1910 and even then it would take some months to establish the personnel and machinery of effective occupation. For most of 1910 the Lado Enclave was therefore an area incredibly rich in animal life (the last part of the continent to have a large elephant population) and devoid of all controls on sportsmen.

It was, truly, a hunter's paradise. In the dry season the herds obligingly concentrated themselves for weeks at a time along the water courses.

'All the elephant for 100 miles inland were crowded into the swamps lining the Nile banks. Hunting was difficult only on account of the high grass. To surmount this one required either a dead elephant or a tripod to stand on. . . . And the best of it was the huge herds were making so much noise themselves that only a few of them could hear the report of the small-bore. None of the elephant could be driven out of the swamp. . . . Later on when the rains came and the green stuff sprang up everywhere—in a night, as it were—scarcely an elephant could be found in the swamps.'

Then the hunter had to pursue the herds towards the primeval forest. Before long he would be rewarded by a heart-warming sight:

'Hundreds upon hundreds of elephant came to feed on the fresh grass. They stood around on that landscape as if made of wood and stuck there. Hunting there was too easy. . . . Soon natives flocked to our camp, and at one time there must have been 3,000 of them . . . when it came to moving our ivory they were indispensable. Without them we could not have budged.'

These were the experiences of another of the legendary sportsmen of Africa, W. D. M. Bell, better known as 'Karamoja' Bell. He had hunted for years in northern Uganda (hence his nickname) and had crossed into the Lado Enclave in the days when it was still under C.F.S. control. His experiences at the hands of Belgian officials are a good indication of why this fabulous elephant country failed to attract many white hunters before 1910. Bell paid £20 for an unrestricted elephant licence, thinking that this would enable him to make free with his rifle during the open season (May–November). He was sadly mistaken. Every C.F.S. post officer was a law unto himself. Bell's piece of paper counted for little to these men, each of whom expected a bribe. Failure to co-operate could have unpleasant consequences:

'. . . some Belgian soldiers met him on the banks of the river and said that the white man wanted to see him up at the fort. Having taken his boots off and left them in the camp on the other side, he said he could not go up just then as he had no boots on, but would come as soon as he got them from the camp.

'Two of the soldiers at once caught hold of the canoe, while a third covered him with his rifle, at the same time calling to the others in Swahili to "come and catch the white man". Knowing the murderous character of the Belgian Native soldiers, Bell did not like being covered in this fashion, as he knew that the men would not hesitate to shoot. He decided to get in the first shot, and, picking up his rifle, winged one of the *askaris*, and pushed off into the middle of the river. By this time the alarm had been given, and about thirty more soldiers came running down from the fort and opened fire with their rifles, but as, fortunately, they were very bad shots, they did not hit him.

'In the meanwhile the white officers had come down from the fort, and all Bell's boys who were on that side of the river were rounded up. The Belgian officers then held a consultation, and decided that as Bell had shot one of their men they must shoot one of his. Taking one of Bell's porters at random they fired a volley into him, and were satisfied that they had squared the matter. They then looted the whole of Bell's property, camp, equipment, guns, ammunition and everything that he had.'

The Lado Enclave was wild, fever-ridden country, inhospitable to white man at the best of times, without his having to take into consideration the opposition of his own kind.

But with the Belgian officials removed, the potential profits were too vast to be ignored and the 'ivory rush' began in earnest.

'Into the Enclave then came this horde. At first they were for the most part orderly, law-abiding citizens, but soon the restraints were thrown off. Finding themselves in a country where even murder went unpunished, every man became a law unto himself. Uganda could not touch him, the Sudan had no jurisdiction for six months, and the Belgians had gone. Some of the men went utterly bad and behaved atrociously to the natives, but the majority were too decent to do anything but hunt elephants. But the few bad men made it uncommonly uncomfortable for the decent ones. The natives became suspicious, disturbed, shy and treacherous. The game was shot at, missed, wounded or killed by all sorts of people who had not the rudiments of hunter-craft or rifle shooting.'

Thus did the Europeans who so heartily condemned the outrageous behaviour of their Arab precursors adopt the same insensitivity to man and beast when goaded by ivory lust.

The newcomers to the Enclave were a motley crew indeed. There was the solitary, eccentric Frenchman who wandered through the jungle without any nether garments, clad only in hat, shirt and boots. He believed in travelling light and sleeping rough; his modest caravan was not encumbered with tents, beds and the other civilised paraphernalia which white men seemed to consider essential to life in the Dark Continent. His rations consisted almost entirely of sugar and absinthe—the former presumably to strengthen him against the rigours of the jungle and the latter to enable him to escape from them. However strange his methods and equipment, he was far from being incompetent with a gun and amassed over a ton of ivory before meeting his end. Perhaps it was inevitable that death should come to him on the tusks of an angry bull elephant.

More typical of the incompetent fortune-seekers who participated in the ivory rush was the Italian hotelier from Uganda. Having for some years catered for the needs of passing hunters and envied them their success he could eventually stand it no longer. He bought himself some guns, shut up the hotel and set off with his reluctant hotel staff to cross the Nile. He soon fell in with some ex-C.F.S. officials, one of whom was a massive, swarthy Swede and another, a less heroic figure, a former *chef de poste*. They agreed to team up, the *chef de poste* electing to look after the company's victuals. They were soon on the track of elephants and decided on a drink to steady their nerves before proceeding to the *battue*:

'... after two or three aperitifs and a bottle of eau-de-vie, the whole outfit, including askaris, marched on the elephants' position. On coming within range, the askaris, who were scattered all over the place, opened fire, which naturally put the elephants in a commotion and running in all directions, the hunters themselves getting all mixed up with the askaris and not knowing what to do next. The Italian took cover down an ant-bear hole; the Swede threw off his tunic and, with his sleeves rolled up, put in some heavy work, letting go at every and any thing he could see; the *Chef de Poste*, seeing an opening in the rear, made for it with his lunch basket, and was not seen again; and the lieutenant and his askaris kept up a heavy fire till there was nothing more in sight.

'After the Italian had come out of the ant-bear hole and the argument had finished as to why he was there, they went to look for the dead elephants; but there were none—and as neither was there any lunch, they parted with mutual recriminations.'

A quite appalling degree of needless suffering was inflicted upon the elephants of the Lado Enclave by hunters lacking skill and experience. John Boyes described how he wounded a fine bull which then escaped into the forest. He followed the animal's tracks for several hours only to come up with it at last in thick undergrowth which did not allow him the opportunity of a carefully aimed shot. Boyes happily fired ten rounds at the poor beast 'in the general area of the head' before finally despatching it. Even that elephant was fortunate compared with a giant bull discovered by W. Buckley, another denizen of the Enclave. This magnificent specimen was leading a herd of cows when Buckley took a shot at it. The bull was badly wounded and the females angrily set upon the hunter. Buckley was chased around for several minutes and by the time the cows broke off the pursuit the bull was being escorted away from danger by other members of his harem. Buckley fired off a few more rounds which only lacerated the elephant's skin before he was once again forced to defend himself from other members of the herd. When the distraction was over the bull had disappeared completely. Though Buckley and his trackers searched for several hours they were unable to distinguish the spoor of the wounded animal from that of the many other elephants in that part of the forest. The wretched creature must have crawled away to die in great pain or to be finished off by some cowardly predator.

The sudden sight of a large herd of elephants bristling with potential wealth often went to the head of a newcomer to the Enclave. C. H. Stigand described his first encounter with elephants *en masse*:

'It was the first time I had been in the middle of a big herd with an unrestricted licence, and I am afraid that I rather let myself go. Fresh herds came surging up out of the grass, and I had an exciting five minutes . . . I believe the only one I hit and did not get was one who fell down and afterwards got up again and went off. At any rate no other blood spoor was found after a minute search by my self and many natives. There was such a seething mass of elephant, however, and I had to fire so quickly, that it was very difficult to tell for certain.'

Not all sportsmen went about their business in this way. The more responsible members of the fraternity dubbed the reckless and indiscriminate 'bang bang hunters' and resented being bracketed with them in the popular mind.

Any fool with a loaded rifle could hit an elephant but to achieve a clean kill demanded skill and patience. No-one gave more attention to the technique of shooting elephants than Karamoja Bell. He believed a knowledge of anatomy was vital to effective hunting and studied with care the carcases and skeletons of dead elephants. In his view the efficient sportsman concerned to inflict the minimum of pain on his quarry should always go for the brain shot. This could be achieved from the front by aiming at a small area between the animal's eyes. This shot could only be successfully achieved at close range (about ten metres) and was, therefore, rather hazardous. The brain could also be reached from the flank by firing at a point just behind the base of the ear. The difficulty here was that an elephant's ears are continuously flapping to and fro. If a brain shot proved impossible Bell recommended the sportsman to aim for the heart but care was called for here as it was easy to miss the heart and pierce the lungs instead, causing the animal an unnecessary lingering death. Bell was fascinated by guns and the techniques of hunting to the end of his life, long after his career as a big game hunter had come to an end. With the new weapons devised in the 1930s and 1940s it became possible to effect an easier clean kill by aiming for the neck, through which all the elephant's vital arteries and nerves pass.

Bell always paid the closest attention to personal fitness, a fact which largely explains why he could handle an ocean going yacht at the age of seventy. Elephant shooting, he said:

'. . . requires a considerable amount of muscle training, especially if there is much offhand or standing shooting. In jungle or high grass most of the shots are delivered from the standing position and to be proficient in this requires training and strengthening of muscles that are not ordinarily much in use. The best way to attain this rifle control is to carry your favourite rifle yourself not only when you are hunting but whenever you go out. Dry shoot it at anything and everything. Do all the exercises you can think of with it. Hold it out at arm's length for as long as you can stick it, first in front, then sideways. Get your muscles thoroughly inured to holding it in any position you may choose. Let your will dominate your body and bring it into subjection.'

Bell had many adventures which tested to the uttermost his skill, fitness and perseverance as well as his humaneness. One occurred when he was hunting in the Enclave on the edge of the great forest. He had shot a solitary bull in a clearing when suddenly there was a terrible sound from among the trees on all sides and a horde of elephants rushed into the clearing, completely surrounding their fallen comrade. They made short, menacing rushes in Bell's direction but were unable to locate him accurately:

'. . . when I got a chance at another bull and fired, I really thought I had done it this time, and the whole lot were coming. So vicious was their appearance, and so determined did they seem as they advanced, that I hurriedly withdrew more deeply into the forest. Looking back, however, I saw that as usual it was mostly bluff, and that they had stopped at the edge of the clearing . . . I approached again to try for another bull. Clumsy white man fashion I made some noise which they heard. A lightning rush by a tall and haggard looking cow right into the stuff from which I was looking at them sent me off again.'

Bell was now facing a series of dilemmas. He wanted to dislodge the herd from its chosen 'citadel' but he did not want to indulge in the wholesale slaughter of cows to achieve this end. He wanted to get at the elephants he had already killed but he did not want to drive the herd into the thick cover of the forest as there were still a number of fine bulls present. He wanted to continue shooting but he did not want to provoke an angry charge which might prove fatal for himself or any of his men.

In the midst of the herd Bell saw a fine tusker and prepared himself for a shot that few hunters would have attempted:

'Just a little dark spot above the ear hole was intermittently uncovered by the heads, ears and trunks of the intervening cows, which were still much agitated. At last I got a clear shot and fired. The image was instantly blacked out by the throw-up of the heads of several cows, as they launched themselves furiously at the shot. I was immediately engaged with three of the nearest, and sufficiently angry with them to stand my ground. I hoped to hustle the herd out of their fighting mood. I had spent days of trouble in this patch of forest. My boys had been chased out and demoralised when they attempted to drive them. I myself had been badly scared once or twice with their barging about, and it was now time to see about it. My shot caught the leading cow in the brain and dropped her slithering on her knees right in the track of the two advancing close to her. One kept on towards me . . . so I gave her a bullet in a non-vital place to turn her. With a shriek she stopped, slewed half round and backed a few steps. Then round came her head again facing towards me. I was on the point of making an end of her when a mass of advancing heads, trunks and ears appeared on both sides of her. From that moment onward I can give no coherent description of what followed, because the images appeared, disappeared and changed with such rapidity as to leave no permanent impression.'

At last the herd was driven from the clearing and Bell was able to collect his ivory. But, as Karamoja admitted, the contest between man and beast on this occasion resulted in a draw. He had gained possession of the glade, 'but as for clearing the patch of forest—no! That was their victory'. It need scarcely be added that many of Bell's contemporaries in the Enclave would have had a field day—shooting at every beast in sight—had they been in his shoes.

In the Lado Enclave there was certainly no excuse for the indiscriminate slaughter of young elephants and females. There were plenty of fine bulls to be found, many of which carried tusks weighing over 100 lb. Under these circumstances careful selection and skilled shooting were usually as rewarding as orgies of undisciplined bang-banging. Yet even to the most skilful hunter luck is an important element in the game. The prize for the luckiest sportsman must surely go to F. G. Banks, one of the Lado Enclave adventurers. He killed three elephants with one shot. It happened like this: Banks shot and killed one beast which, in falling, stumbled against two companions. All three elephants toppled over the edge of a cliff and were discovered dead at the bottom.

The Lado Enclave was a land of humid climate, marsh, tall grass, mosquitoes and swollen rivers. In such a country the white man was dependent on local people for the success and sometimes for the very survival of his expedition. The Africans provided food and porters. They located elephant herds and sometimes even rounded up elephants and drove them towards the hunter's ambush. Usually all they required in return was elephant meat. Frequently dead elephants would be left lying where they had fallen as the sportsman went on to pursue other quarry. He would return at the end of the day to find that the local people had stripped the meat from the carcases and either left the ivory or carried it to his camp. They would not have dreamed of stealing the tusks for fear of bringing to an end a very profitable partnership.

Many visitors were moved by the enormous hospitality offered by African chiefs, a hospitality based on proud custom and not self-interest. Coming on a river in flood, C. H. Stigand sent for help to the leader of a village on the other side. The chief turned out all his young men to ferry Stigand's loads across the water. Last of all he transported the hunter and set him safely on the opposite shore. Stigand immediately opened one of his bales to offer the chief some calico in payment but the old man waved it aside and beckoned the white man to enter his village. It was, says Stigand, 'the poorest village I had ever set eyes on. The few hovels consisted of some poles with a little grass thrown over the top'. Yet the chief rushed into his house to return with a scrawny chicken which he urged Stigand to accept. Etiquette demanded that the host should offer the first present. Stigand was not alone in discovering that, even in places where the people were too poor to be able to offer food for sale, the civil exchange of gifts was insisted upon.

In these circumstances ill treatment of the Africans was not only morally indefensible; it was the height of folly. But the 'bang bang hunters' did not take this into account. All that concerned them was getting the maximum amount of ivory in the shortest possible time. They paid for African 'co-operation' with threats, violence and trickery, often behaving no better than the old Arab slavers whose dealings had been so roundly condemned by Europe. By and large the African on his own territory was more than a match for bothersome white men. As a guide he could become incredibly stupid even to the point of 'losing' the track only a stone's throw from his own village. He could 'forget' which way elephants had gone and send the anxious hunter in entirely the wrong direction. Sometimes he had more humorous ways of registering a protest. One chief reluctantly agreed to send some of his men up the Nile with Stigand to help the white man get his ivory home. But he took exception to the hunter's manner as Stigand discovered when he checked the new porters onto the steamer which was to transport them upriver:

'There was some delay about getting off, and just as I thought everything was ready, I saw the sergeant, who was accompanying me, cross the gangway carrying a man in his arms. I imagined that it was a sick man being brought for medicine or dressing and was rather annoyed that our journey should be delayed. I waited patiently for him to be brought up to me on the upper deck, but no-one came and presently the sergeant reported that all was ready to start.

'I asked him who it was that he had carried on board. "Was it not one of master's porters from chief so-and-so?" he replied. I went down to inspect the man and found that he was a paralytic cripple who could not walk. He had been selected by his chief as a porter for me.'

Stigand put the selection down to stupidity on the part of the chief. He was neither the first nor the last thick-skinned white man to refuse to take a hint.

Some communities were goaded beyond endurance by the arrogance and brutality of the get-rich-quick ivory speculators. They began to reply in kind and within a few months of the start of the rush certain areas had become notoriously dangerous for white men. For a start the people quickly discovered just how valuable the big, curved elephant teeth were. They began to demand higher prices for ivory and for assistance given to the hunters. Elephant meat was no longer sufficient; they wanted trade goods and, above all, guns. Thus equipped they made themselves a menace along the trade trails. On his way out of the Enclave with his great haul of ivory Buckley had the misfortune to find himself in the country of the much feared Lugwara:

'While busy on the camp I found these people unduly friendly—from my experience a distinctly bad sign—and pestering me as to what things they could bring me for a present . . . If I wanted eggs away went four or five people to get them, and so with other things also. They asked me if I wanted beer. I told them no, but the beer arrived just the same, six large calabashes full, another suspicious circumstance, as natives as a rule do not throw their beer about in this manner. I suspected moreover that it was drugged, the quantity being obviously much more than I should need for myself, and their idea being that I would give it to the gunbearers and porters. However, I did nothing of the kind, but kicked the stuff over when nobody was about.

'I could clearly see that under this ostentatious friendship there was mischief, as I had by this time a pile of eggs about two feet high, and I had already remonstrated with them about bringing so much food, telling them that I was unable to carry it. To prevent them bringing any more I had for some time ceased to give them any payment for what they had brought up, which, in an ordinary way, would have effectually stopped it, but with no stopping these people, I came to the conclusion that they were only loaning them to me and counted on getting them all back. Nor was my guide, a small youth, deceived by this outward show of friendliness —with tears in his eyes averring that we were all as good as dead meat . . .

'Another extremely suspicious circumstance had occurred just previously, two Lugwara natives having asked me to sign them on as porters. I had never heard of this tribe taking to any sort of work, especially the job of carrying loads, so, not to make them think that I tumbled to what they were after, I took out my book and solemnly signed them on. When I ordered all the natives out of camp these two wanted to remain, ostensibly to carry my loads in the morning, but really, of course, to act as spies. I told them that that was impossible, they being of a different tribe to the others, and so could not occupy the same tent; to which they could offer no objection and left rather disappointed.

'. . . the natives having all gone home and the porters having cooked and eaten their food . . . I called up the gunbearers, the cook and the guide, and, to their immense relief, gave orders to march at once. My tent was pulled down without the slightest noise and packed, and when everything was ready the porters were summoned and told on no account to speak, but quietly to gather up their loads and leave their fires burning. The night was pitch dark, no moon or stars showing.

'Adjuring the porters not to lose touch with each other or they would be irretrievably lost and killed by the shenzis, we started, the small guide with his feet on the footpath facing south, so that he could feel the track although he could not see it. Where there were branching tracks he was to signal me to that effect, and I would then get down to the ground and by striking matches and the aid of a compass would indicate which path he was to follow.

'We travelled in this manner till just on three o'clock in the morning, losing half the safari at one period of the night, and fortunately, by means of whistling, etc., managing to round them all up again. It was extremely awkward travelling, as every now and again we would bump into a village, whereupon my guide—always first to see them—would whistle softly and we would make a detour to avoid awakening the inhabitants. We were on ploughed land . . . and with no possibility of the natives we had left being able to track us, I gave the order to halt and put loads down and sleep . . .

'At the first streak of dawn, awaking the sleeping safari, I observed through the gathering daylight that every ant-hill in the distance had one or two natives on top peering for our safari, quite enough evidence to convince me that they had been at the old camp during the night to find the birds flown.'

For the survivors the dangers and rigours of the Enclave were well worthwhile. Probably more ivory fortunes were made

in a few months there than in any other part of Africa. Walter
Bell shot 210 elephants in nine months and took from them
over five tons of ivory. John Boyes made three forays into the
Enclave in 1910. On each of the two earlier trips he came out
with about half a ton of tusks. By the time he set out on his
last safari the orgy was nearly over; it was but a few weeks to
the establishment of British jurisdiction. Boyes decided to
grab all the ivory he could. He obtained so much that he had
great difficulty getting it out of the country. At last he had to
transport his horde from village to village, hiring porters for
short haul journeys as he went along. Chauncey Stigand ran
into a similar problem. Not having enough porters to carry his
ivory back to 'civilisation', he decided to make part of the
journey by canoe. Unfortunately, his men had come from a
non-riverain community; they knew nothing about canoeing
and were terrified of crocodiles. With patient persistence which
did not come easily to him Stigand had to teach his followers
how to propel and manipulate canoes—it was either that or
leave the bulk of his ivory behind.

If the Lado Enclave made some men wealthy it took a
deadly toll of others. Some fell victim to malaria or blackwater
fever. Some were killed by elephants. This could happen to the
most skilful and experienced hunters. The wild elephant is a
dangerous, clever and unpredictable adversary and a mere
momentary lack of caution on the part of the sportsman may
prove fatal. After many years of successful hunting a German
made the mistake of walking up to a recumbent bull believing
it to be an animal he had mortally wounded the previous day.
He was actually examining the tusks when the creature, which
had been dozing, felled him with a wave of its trunk and
transfixed his body with a tusk. Some hunters fell victim to
Africans whom they had unnecessarily antagonised. One
sportsman fell out with a community living on the edge of the
Congo forest over the issue of some milk he wanted for a young
rhinoceros he had captured. As a result he was ambushed by
warriors and died an unpleasant death:

'At the first attack he received the charge from an old
muzzle-loading rifle in his thigh, severing one of the arteries.
He fell at once but continued to keep off his assailants while

lying on the ground . . . while he lay there bleeding to death, he accounted for no fewer than thirteen of his enemies . . . the Natives finally rushed in on the wounded man and hacked him to pieces, cutting off his head and otherwise mutilating him.'

Other white men had fatal encounters with crocodiles and hippos while ferrying their precious ivory across one or other of the innumerable water courses flowing towards the Nile or the Congo. This part of Africa held many dangers for the stranger. Those who blundered into the Enclave and showed no respect for the country or its inhabitants did so at their peril.

But for the true hunter it was the thrill of the chase and the camaraderie of the camp fire which drew him to the Enclave as to any other area in which he hunted. It is therefore fitting to end this chapter with another anecdote from the memoirs of Karamoja Bell, which conveys the good-humoured comradeship which the sportsman and his colleagues enjoyed on safari.

'At camp, close to the edge of the great forest, I was sitting on a little hill one evening. Along one of the innumerable elephant paths I saw a small bull coming. Suliemani, my faithful servant and cook, had for years boasted how he would kill elephant if he were given the chance. Here it was, and I should be able to see the fun. I came down to camp, called for Suliemani, gave him a rifle and thirty rounds, pointed out to him the direction of the elephant, and sent him off. Then I reclimbed the hill from which I could see both Suliemani and the elephant. The bull, having perhaps caught a whiff of our camp, had turned and was now leisurely making towards the forest. Soon Suliemani got his tracks and went racing along behind him. The elephant now entered some long grass which had escaped the fire, and this stuff evidently hid him from Suliemani's view. At the time it was not sufficiently high to prevent my seeing what happened through my glasses. In the high grass the elephant halted and Suliemani came slap into him. With two frightful starts Suliemani turned and fled in one direction, the elephant in the other. After half a hundred yards Suliemani pulled himself together and once more took up the trail, disappearing into the forest. Soon shot after shot was heard. There was no lack of friends in camp to count the number poor Suliemani fired. When twenty-seven had been heard there was silence for a long time. Darkness fell, everyone supped. Then came Suliemani stalking empty-handed into camp. A successful hunter always cuts off the tail and brings it home. Suliemani had failed after all his blowing. The camp was filled with jeers and jibes. Not a word from Suliemani as he prepared to eat his supper. Having eaten it in silence, the whole time being ragged to death by his mates, he quietly stepped across the camp, disappeared a moment into the darkness, and re-appeared with the elephant's tail. He had killed it after all! There was a shout of laughter, but all Suliemani said was, "Of course".'

8

'He did not know that a keeper is only a poacher turned outside in, and a poacher a keeper turned inside out.'

—Charles Kingsley, THE WATER BABIES

Poachers and Keepers

The spread of effective colonial rule considerably curtailed the activities of elephant hunters, both African and European. Animal reserves were designated where hunting was totally forbidden and in other areas the conditions under which shooting licences were awarded were tightened up. Those who were unwilling to leave their life of adventure thus became poachers. Those who traded in their freedom for an official badge became keepers and, as we shall see, often found they had greater opportunities than ever before for hunting elephants. There were a few Europeans who occupied a midway position. These were the 'white hunters' who obtained their thrills by selling their experience and skills to wealthy patrons who came to Africa for holiday safaris. There were many famous names among these patrons, including the Prince of Wales, President Theodore Roosevelt, Winston Churchill and Ernest Hemingway.

Most of Africa's game parks were created in the period between and after the two world wars but the idea was not a twentieth-century invention. The man who started the elephant conservation movement back in the 1880s was Paul Kruger, later to become President of the Transvaal Republic and leader of the Boers. He had been a first class hunter in his youth and he became increasingly dismayed at the rate at which elephants faded from the newly opened up areas of the high veld. In 1884 he proposed to the Transvaal parliament the creation of national reserves. Nothing came of this but he continued to urge his case and in 1888 a resolution of his, calling for the establishment of sanctuaries to preserve some parts of the country in their original state was accepted. But it was not acted upon. Kruger continued his fight and in 1894 the small Pongola Reserve became the first animal sanctuary in Africa. This was a small beginning but the precedent had been established and the way was paved for a further advance. On 6th September 1895 a new resolution was passed by the Transvaal Parliament:

'The undersigned, seeing that nearly all big game in the Republic have been exterminated, and that those animals still remaining are becoming less day by day, so that there is a danger of them becoming altogether extinct in the near future, request to be permitted to depart from the order paper to discuss the desirability of authorising the government to proclaim as a Government Game Reserve, where killing of game shall altogether be prohibited, certain portions of the district of Lydenburg being Government land, where most of the big game species are still to be found, to wit, the territory situated between the Crocodile and the Sabi rivers with the boundaries as follows . . .'

The new park was formed on 26th March 1898 and was known as the Sabi Game Reserve. Later a second area called Shingwedzi, quite close to it was also reserved. Finally in 1926 the two were joined by the inclusion of the land between to make one vast area some 7,000 square miles in extent. Appropriately this vast conservation area was named the Kruger National Park.

The Sabi Reserve was not properly staffed until after the Anglo-Boer War of 1899–1901 but then a full time game warden, the first in the world, was appointed. The choice could not have been a better one. James Stevenson-Hamilton had been a keen hunter in his youth and, like most successful hunters, was a first class naturalist. He held the post from July 1902 until he retired in 1946 having pioneered a whole new approach to game conservation and set a pattern to be repeated in many other countries with valuable wildlife resources.

When Kruger National Park was first reserved it contained only ten elephant. The huge herds which had roamed the whole of Southern Africa since time immemorial had been reduced to this pitiful remnant together with the small herd at Addo near the Cape. As soon as the area was enclosed however, the population became resurgent and now there are as many elephant in the area as it can hold without damage. This has been achieved partly by the entry of new stock from the hunting areas of Mozambique to the west and partly by the naturally high reproductive rate of elephants when undisturbed by man.

South Africa was at least forty years ahead of the rest of the continent in the development of game reserves but the success of Kruger National Park in restoring to some extent the balance upset by generations of ivory hunters was a spur to the development of the conservation idea. Today there are well over a hundred game parks throughout Africa. The principal reserves dedicated to elephant conservation are as follows, the dates (where available) in brackets indicating the first opening of the park:

South Africa:	Addo Elephant Reserve (1931)
	Kruger National Park (1898)
South-West Africa:	Etosha Pan Nature Reserve (1928)
Rhodesia:	Victoria Falls National Park (1952)
	Wankie National Park (1950)
Zambia:	Kafue National Park (1950)
	Lukusuzi Game Reserve (1942)
	Sumbu Game Reserve (1942)
Malawi:	Kota Kota Game Reserve
Mozambique:	Limpopo Game Reserve
Zaire:	Albert National Park (1929)
	Upemba National Park (1939)
Angola:	Egito Reserve
	Mupa Reserve
Tanzania:	Serengeti National Park (1940)
	Ngorongoro Conservation Area (1959)
	Kilimanjaro Reserve (1914)
	Lake Manyara Reserve (1957)
	Selous Reserve (1914)
Kenya:	Aberdare National Park (1950)
	Tsavo National Park (1948)
	Samburu National Park (1950)

Uganda: Murchison Falls National Park (1952)
                   Queen Elizabeth National Park (1952)
                   Toro Game Reserve (1946)
                   Bugungu Hippopotamus and Elephant
                   Sanctuary

It can be seen from the dates in this list that the conservation snowball gathered momentum very slowly; by far the greater number of reserves did not come into being until the period 1945–60. There were many reasons for this but the principal one was the enormity of the problem. Vast areas had to be fenced and policed; herd movements had to be carefully observed; transport and communication over long distances of trackless country were difficult to establish. Further to that, in years of war and economic crisis problems of human geography presented the administrators of young colonies with quite enough problems; wildlife conservation, though the passionate concern of many officials, was not a high priority in imperial budgets.

The problem of endangered species was fully recognised, however. In 1900 representatives of Britain, France, Germany, Portugal, the Congo Free State, Italy and Spain signed a convention 'for the preservation of wild animals, birds and fish in Africa' but the document was never ratified by individual governments and the initiative was left with individual colonial administrations to bring in and enforce their own regulations. For many years poachers were thus able to play off one authority against another. If one country was getting too 'hot' for them they could skip across a frontier into the territory of a more amenable or less efficient regime. Not until 1933 was effective international co-operation on wildlife protection achieved. In that year the International Conference for the Protection of the Fauna and Flora of Africa was convened in London. The result was a convention finally ratified by all the colonial governments in 1936. It provided for full co-operation on the siting of conservation areas, common policies on the restriction of hunting and tighter controls on the export of trophies, principally ivory.

What was good news for the animals was a message of doom for the white hunters. We need not shed too many tears for the passing of what had been a fine, free way of life for a privileged, if brave, minority. Yet something irreplaceable had departed from the world and, as one ex-hunter tried to say in verse, one of the few places where a man could find adventure was now closed to men of spirit:

'Now, though the world is just as wide, though herds are
    still the same,
Though seas of grasses still divide before the rush of game,
From "British East" to "German West" from Congo to
    Koroo,
There is no gap to fail the test and let the hunter through,
"Thou shalt not kill the elephant"—so runs the Law today—
Hang up the battered bandolier, the Ring-Fence bars the
    way.

Hang up the battered bandolier and let the rifle rust,
For now the dreams of yesteryear and all they held in trust
Must take the place of strenuous days and starlit nights of
    old,
Of morning mists and noontide blaze and weariness and
    cold . . .
No more the Tusker of those dreams shall charge, with
    trunk encurled,
No more, at dawn, thou'lt pace the paths with dancing
    dew empearled . . .
No more crouch low and test the wind . . . the Ring-Fence
    hems the world.'

If the imperial presence had for many of the old school of ivory hunters ruined the Africa they knew and loved, for the new breed of sportsman the extra risk of being caught by the game department added a dash of spice to the business of shooting elephants. But a poacher's life had its problems and though it might bring an abundance of adventure it was unlikely to make a man rich. Ivory sold on the underworld market fetched only a half of the prevailing auction room price and the tusks had to be conveyed usually over difficult country to the secret rendezvous where the dealers came to collect it. The hunter had to know a wide tract of country very well. He needed to know where unmarked administrative borders ran so that he could, when necessary, convey himself and his ivory into the territory of a 'co-operative' *chef de poste*. He had to study the seasonal movements of the game, for he lived completely off the land and his livelihood depended on his ability to find and kill elephants on a regular basis. The poacher was more ruthless and undiscriminating than the man hunting under licence. He could not afford to be scrupulous about immature and cow elephants: any beast that carried ivory was his prey. The poacher often found that time was not on his side. A herd moving towards the territory of a particularly vigilant game warden must be attacked before it got too close to safety. The tusks of a dead elephant frequently had to be cut out at great speed; the excitement of the local people coming for the meat would soon attract the attention of the authorities. The illicit hunter had to know which chiefs he could trust and which he could not. He had to know of convenient hiding places where ivory could be concealed in a hurry.

Above all, the poacher needed a base camp well sited in dense bush or forest which was safe from discovery. G. G. Rushby who hunted Mozambique, Tanganyika, Northern Rhodesia and Congo in the 1920s and 1930s sited his headquarters:

'. . . at a well hidden spot in the Belgian Congo about five miles from the border. It was near the old slave route running from Pweto on Lake Mweru to Moliro on Lake Tanganyika. This route was still well defined in places and had been used by the notorious Arab slaver Tippu Tip. This was the first section of the long journey along which the slave gangs had struggled laden with ivory on their way to Moliro, Lake Tanganyika, Ujiji, Tabora, Bagamoyo and the short sea crossing to the slave markets of Zanzibar.

'On the Rhodesian side of the border my nearest neighbours were two petty chiefs, Tambala and Sirimani. Tambala, a large fat elderly man, had been a soldier of Tippu Tip and was wounded at the battle for the slavers' fort at Pweto, . . . Sirimani claimed to be a son of Tippu Tip by an African mother . . . These two men became my two chief intelligence officers and they built up a network of informers that covered the whole of that section of Northern Rhodesia. It was largely due to the efficiency of the organisation that I had so little difficulty avoiding the patrols sent out by the administrative authorities of Mporocoso and Chienji to apprehend me.'

The poachers could usually rely on the support of the local people. The white hunter was still a good supplier of meat so that the villagers had every reason to assist him and very little incentive to help the authorities capture him. Not that Rushby had any difficulty with the Belgian officials; the local *chef de poste* turned a very blind eye towards his activities. It was the persistence of the Rhodesians that eventually put a stop to his hunting in that area:

'. . . the Rhodesian authorities, having failed in their efforts to apprehend me, made representations to the Belgian Administrative Officer at Moliro about my activities. The Administrative Officer sent me a letter by runner and suggested I come into Moliro to discuss the position with him. This I did, and he advised me to stop my poaching operations and leave the area for if the complaints went to higher authorities he would have no option but to hand me over to the Rhodesian authorities.'

Rushby was very sorry to leave. He had discovered in the marshy area around Lake Mweru what must have been the last great elephant hunting ground in Africa. Because of the abundance of animal life there the government of Northern Rhodesia had designated the Mweru Marsh a game reserve. Such formalities were of little interest to the poacher. Rushby enjoyed a six-month hunting spree amidst the tall grasses and papyrus of the marsh. On his best day he shot eighteen elephants, all but two of which were bulls.

John Taylor, who also began his poaching career in the 1920s, made his headquarters in Mozambique. After some close shaves with an 'over-zealous' *chef de poste* Taylor decided to put his activities on a legal footing and took out a game licence. This did not signify a change of heart; it simply provided Taylor with a secure economic basis for his business and a safe refuge in time of trouble. It enabled him, as he said, 'to hunt the Portuguese elephant legally and have the three British frontiers

—the Rhodesias and Nyasaland, to say nothing of Tanganyika if I made my way as far north as that—over which to poach if I were not satisfied with the number of elephant allowed on my licence'. Taylor took full advantage of the difficulties experienced by overworked and understaffed game departments and was able on more than one occasion to carry out prolonged and highly organised raids into forbidden territory. One such was across the Rovuma river into southern Tanganyika:

'There were plenty of elephant on my side of the river. There was absolutely no necessity for me to cross into British territory. But I had a notion to indulge in the time-honoured pastime of tweaking the lion's tail . . .

'I had persuaded a friend, Sherif, an African-Arab and the world's champion smuggler, to bring his dhow into the mouth of the Rovuma to ensure a clean getaway with my ivory— just in case. He had taken on board all the ivory I had collected over quite a considerable period on more or less legitimate hunting. Now, with his dhow tied up in a backwater and well camouflaged, he was to act as my base during the raid . . .

'Since all natives who had previously lived in what was to become the reserve had been removed by the British when it was made a reserve, a poacher had to carry with him all the food that he and his men might require. And since porters must naturally eat their share of what they are carrying, my method was to have a string of porters bring all the food I and my "flying squad" would want for, say, ten days or so, dump it in a place I had chosen for a bivouac for the period in question and return to base. After the stipulated time they would come back to where they had left us, bringing more food, and would take away all ivory shot during their absence. I would then move out another ten or fifteen or twenty miles to another centre around which to shoot, and that is where the men would come with supplies next time. Depending on the conditions it might be a week's or a month's supplies they brought; but when poaching in some pet reserve, I liked the men to return at not-too-distant intervals so as to make sure I would get a fair share of whatever ivory I shot. Otherwise I might have to leave in a hurry, abandoning all the fruits of perhaps a month's hunting . . . My flying squad consisted of half a dozen specially picked men, all young, strong fellows, tough and fit and game for anything. I never loaded these men heavily, so we could and frequently did cover over thirty, thirty-five and forty miles a day, sometimes for days and days on end.'

In northern Kenya and Uganda the problems faced by the poacher were different. Effective colonial rule was not extended over these areas until well into the 1920s. Karamoja and the Northern Frontier District of Kenya were, like the neighbouring areas of Ethiopia and the Sudan still overrun by Egyptian, Ethiopian, Swahili, Sudanese and European ivory and slave traders. In defiance of all authority, native and imperial, the marauders wrought havoc among the human and animal populations of a large part of Africa. Henry Darley, while growing rich on the proceeds of unrestricted ivory hunting, had many narrow escapes during the first quarter of the twentieth century which he spent in this savage no-man's land. In 1910 he helped to resist an Ethiopian takeover of Turkana, Karamoja and Suk. On another occasion he was put on trial in an Ethiopian court, charged with mass murder. His store of ivory was a constant temptation to warring Ethiopian and Galla bands. Frequently he found himself the only representative of the very colonial authority he was so openly defying, an ironical state of affairs which he savoured fully:

'I used to smile to myself to think that here was I, who had been considered to be an ivory poacher of the worst sort, whom every game warden in British East Africa and Uganda must have longed to lay his hands on, keeping the peace and saving a large area of the territory their administration was supposed to govern, from spoilation and even actual occupation by a neighbouring power.'

There is little reason to doubt that but for the unofficial activities of adventurers like Darley many boundaries on the map of colonial Africa would have eventually been drawn rather differently.

White poachers were never slow in providing justification for their activities. If they could not pose as preservers of the *Pax*

Britannica they portrayed themselves as protectors of the African livelihood. Again, there was an element of truth in this claim. As John Taylor pointed out: 'elephants don't remain peacefully in reserves all the year round. They break out and go raiding wherever they think they can get away with it . . . I have seen what happens. And although I am fond of those big grey ghosts of the forest, as I look at it man, be he black, white, brown or brindled, is deserving of greater consideration than elephant.' No doubt the poacher was for many African communities the only prospect of speedy salvation when marauding elephants trampled their shambas, uprooted their crops and destroyed their fences.

The problem of damage done by elephants was a real one and white hunters were the first to point out that conservation was making it worse. As the elephant populations within the reserves grew they soon consumed all the readily available foodstuff. Then they wandered out of the protected areas in search of sustenance. The immediate answer conceived by the British authorities was the British Elephant Control Scheme: a few white hunters with a force of well-trained Africans stalked the areas contiguous to the reserves destroying animals that had strayed into places where they could cause trouble. This stop-gap measure had many drawbacks. It takes a herd of elephant on the move very little time indeed to turn fertile land into a wilderness which may not recover for many seasons. Anyone driving through Tsavo Game Park in Kenya today cannot help noticing that the area looks as though two warring armies have recently passed through. Most of the trees have been knocked over and are lying on their sides, leafless and dead; the giant bottle shaped Baobabs, so typical of these dry plains, have had their trunks ripped open as though by explosions. This is the work of the elephant. Although Tsavo is over 8,000 square miles in extent, the majority of the land has become a semi-desert. The elephant population in the park must consume something of the order of 7,000 tons of fodder each day in order to survive. In the dry season when leafy shoots are in short supply these powerful beasts become desperate, they knock over trees in order to reach the last little bit of leaf and use their tusks to break open the trunks of softer, juicier trees such as the Baobab. There can be no question of survival for human beings or other species in the wake of a herd of hungry elephants.

Even if the official British croppers could have dealt swiftly with every marauding elephant that would not have been an end of the problem. Herds not infrequently passed into neighbouring colonial territories such as Mozambique where the government was less well organised to deal with the problem. The Portuguese officials made little or no attempt to safeguard their colonial subjects from the devastations of wandering elephants. The elephants were quick to learn where the 'safe' areas were and thousands of them crossed over into 'Portuguese East'.

One service which African and European poachers performed for the elephant was in forcing the colonial governments to realise that conservation was not a simple business of designating reserves. When the idea of sanctuaries for wild animals was promulgated by Paul Kruger and others, very little was known of the complications of ecology. It was thought that if an area was set aside, in a perfectly 'wild' state (i.e. with no human interference) the animals would live there for ever as they seemed to have done in the past. Unfortunately, like man, no game park is an island. No matter how large it is there is a constant interaction round its boundaries, and game animals, especially elephants, are never static. The ecology of any area is a dynamic thing, it can never be kept still except by human interference.

Conservation could have very unfortunate effects on the human ecology of a region. It made poachers of communities for whom hunting had always been an integral part of life. For many centuries the Liangulu of southern Kenya had lived on the elephants migrating from the swampy regions of the Tana river district to the north through to Kilimanjaro and the Serengeti plains. They had developed for this work a technique demanding both skill and strength. Their unique and tremendously powerful bows had a pull of over 100 lb. and from them the Liangulu fired an iron-headed arrow tipped with Acokanthera poison. Within their tribal culture the whole elephant was used, the skin, meat and tusks. At the beginning of the twentieth century the traditional pattern of life began to change. The Liangulu were influenced by traders from the coast, who bought tusks in exchange for alcohol and drugs

such as bhang. As a result of the incessant encouragement
and demand of these traders the Liangulu used their efficient
methods to kill large numbers of elephant for the sake of the
tusks alone. The rest of the animal was left to rot. The elephant
population declined rapidly. Throughout East and Central
Africa the twentieth century witnessed a decimation of the
elephant herds far more critical than any seen before. African
peoples such as the Liangulu were responsible for much more
of this slaughter than white hunters. The Liangulu found it very
difficult to understand the hostility of the game department to
their activities. Had not the white man and the coast Swahili
always encouraged them to hunt for ivory?

Matters were made worse when the Tsavo area, their traditional hunting ground, was made into a national park in 1947.
Now the killing of even one elephant was illegal. But how could
the Liangulu stop hunting? They depended upon the ivory they
sold at the coast for their alcohol and drugs. What could they
know of the white man's law, these people who had lived and
hunted the area for their whole tribal history without affecting
it in any way?

Naturally enough the Liangulu continued to hunt the elephant in their own traditional way and in their own traditional
hunting grounds. The pity of it was that they did not hunt their
own traditional amounts. In order to supply the demands of
illegal traders they began to slaughter the animals in the newly
set up sanctuary of the national park. One group of hunters
was reported to have killed 3,000 elephant in a little over two
years. Slaughter on this scale in a national park could not be
allowed to continue and the park authorities under the Warden,
Mr David Sheldrick, set up a military style organisation to
combat the poachers. A force was created which included men
and machinery from the National Parks administration, from
the Game Department and also from the Police. The Liangulu
stood little chance against such opposition; within about two
years 'poaching' by the Liangulu had more or less stopped. The
hunting gangs and the trading syndicates at the coast had been
broken up and most of the male Liangulu were in jail.

This could not be the end of the story. A permanent solution
had to be found for these people whose whole life depended
upon hunting, especially upon hunting elephant. In order to

assist them the Galana Game Management Scheme was started in the area. The Liangulu were encouraged to manage their area (outside the Tsavo boundary) on a more scientific basis and sublimate their hunting instinct by collecting meat and trophies for sale. On paper the idea was a good one; in practice it did not work well. The Kenya government insisted that the revenue from the sale of trophies from the scheme should be channelled into General Revenue as is normal in such cases; none was to be retained by the Liangulu. There was thus little incentive for the mighty elephant slayers to co-operate. Understandably, the Liangulu gradually lost interest in the scheme and returned to their old way of life. Today the Liangulu still poach elephant on a large scale. The only slender achievement of the anti-poaching campaign was that it made the people wary of the National Park and they are now careful not to enter it.

The case of the Liangulu is not unique. Every game park which has been founded has caused the displacement of the local peoples' hunting areas. Their livelihood has been taken away from them and nothing has been done to replace it (even if this were possible). Consequently every game sanctuary has a poaching problem. Nor is the problem a small one. To give some idea of the carnage involved it has been estimated that on the mainland of Tanganyika in 1962, some 14,000 animals were legally shot under licence but a conservative estimate was that at least 150,000 more were killed illegally, that is by poaching.

Another cause for concern is the methods used by African hunters. The traditional techniques perfected over centuries were efficient. They also preserved the spirit of the true hunter in that they called for great bravery, skill and patience. In 1954 C. A. W. Guggisberg spent some time with the Bamboti pygmy people of the dense Ituri Forest of the Congo basin. He was shown how they killed the forest elephant of that region by crawling under the unsuspecting beast and pushing a short, broad bladed spear up into its belly:

'When I asked the pygmies if such an audacious way of tackling elephants did not lead to a number of accidents, one of them grinned, pulled down his loincloth and revealed two big, ugly scars, one on each side of his belly. "An elephant did this," somebody said, and it was easy to see that the thin, downward pointing tusks of the forest elephant had been pushed deep into the little man's body. It seemed truly miraculous for him to have recovered from such terrible wounds—but here he stood, hale and hearty.'

Little had occurred in the area to change their way of life since G. G. Rushby had visited them thirty years before. Then they were 'a happy, contented people who had no wish for any other way of life. It is to be hoped that no other way will be forced on them by misguided do-gooders who may happen to be in authority.'

The Bamboti are still protected by their thick forests from undue influences; it has not been so for most of Africa's people. One of the most pernicious influences has been firearms—and inferior firearms at that. Both Arabs and Europeans were guilty of selling muzzle-loading rifles to their African trading partners to encourage them to go out and kill more elephants. Much has been written about the appalling effects of this on the people themselves—the increase of slave raiding, of inter-community and internecine strife. Another terrible result of the use of these weapons was the degree of suffering inflicted on game animals. The guns with which most Africans were equipped were only capable of killing cleanly if handled with great skill at fairly close range. In their eagerness to obtain ivory most African hunters preferred to fire repeatedly into the head and body of their prey. Thousands of elephants died slowly and in great agony as a result. Thousands more escaped to bear wounds and scars for the rest of their lives. Others again were turned from placid creatures into aggressive monsters who would attack any human being they encountered. In all his years in Africa Henry Darley only once suffered an un-provoked charge from an elephant. After he had killed it he discovered that it was peppered all over with gunshot wounds. Nor is the problem an historical one: in Tanzania today over 160,000 old muzzle-loading rifles are licensed by the government.

Yet can one blame the inefficient African hunter for poaching? Outside the game reserves there are catchment areas which are rich in animal life. Until recently these areas were divided up into large blocks where hunting was encouraged for those rich enough to pay for shooting licences. Where local peoples were not allowed to kill for meat the animals in their own areas as they have done for many generations, rich men from overseas who knew and cared little about the place, hunted for trophies merely for 'show'. The foreigners wasted large quantities of meat and skin. It is small wonder that poaching has grown into an enormous problem. The local population, unable to afford an enormous supply of valuable protein food which they knew how to catch, had to watch rich foreigners come for a few days, living in the greatest luxury and obviously not needing game meat for survival, shoot up the herds, then go away again with their spoils.

If blame is to be placed anywhere it must be upon the extremely well padded shoulders of the Arab, Swahili and Asian entrepreneurs who have for generations organised and made great profits from the illicit trade in ivory. The system for smuggling ivory out of Africa was sophisticated and flexible. Dealers (usually shopkeepers) in the interior bought the tusks from black and white poachers. Europeans would be offered between a half and a quarter of the current legitimate market price; Africans usually much less. The ivory, together with skins and rhinoceros horn found its way to the coast by a variety of routes—in canoes, in the boots of cars, in lorries under sacks of vegetables, even by train disguised as bales of cloth. At the coast they might be crated up, falsely labelled and loaded quite openly onto dhows or they might be conveyed to small creeks and inlets to be loaded onto vessels under cover of darkness. The dhows' owners were usually involved in a two way smuggling business, bringing into the country liquor, tobacco, sugar and other dutiable items.

In July 1968 a mixed force of Kenya Game Department officials and police, acting on information received as a result of several months' detective work, raided a warehouse in Mombasa. They opened up crates of 'Jaggery' (a sugar product) ostensibly from Uganda and found an estimated £52,000 worth of trophies, mainly ivory. This huge cargo was destined for the Persian Gulf. This single consignment, roughly equal to the total sales at the Mombasa ivory room for a whole year, was just one that happened to be caught. How many got away?

Not all African poachers were bungling, ill-equipped amateurs. There were a few who had learned their craft well, had good guns and knew how to use them. For years the Tanganyika Game Department's principal enemies were Saidi Chamwenyewe and Huseini Asmani, hunters who were far more successful over a long period than any white men. The authorities knew these two miscreants well and knew exactly what they were up to. Unfortunately Saidi and Huseini were as expert at concealing and disposing of their ivory as they were at killing elephants. No major crime was ever pinned on either of them.

Most white hunters sooner or later went 'legitimate'. Even in his most flagrant exploits the wise poacher was careful not to antagonise the authorities of all the territories in which he operated. As G. G. Rushby said, 'I killed few elephants in Tanganyika in subsequent years, except under licence. One reason for this was that I considered Tanganyika the best of all the territories in tropical Africa and I intended to make my home there should professional elephant hunting ever become uneconomic or no longer possible. For this reason I thought it advisable to have a clean record in the country!' For a time professional hunting did become uneconomic. During the Depression of 1929–33 the price of ivory which had previously stood at 20–25 shillings a pound fell back to only 4–5 shillings. It was at this point that the majority of sportsmen left the country, or took up farming or joined the game departments.

All the British colonies in East and Central Africa had to face up to the problems created by the conservation of elephants during the 1920s. The obvious immediate need was for some form of control and for this the game departments turned to the professional hunters. First of all they tempted the sportsmen with extended licences. In 1923, for example, the Tanganyika Game Department offered hunters licences to kill twenty-five elephants each in certain clearly defined areas. Half the ivory was to go to the department and the other half to the hunter. This had only a limited effectiveness; the hunters obviously went for the biggest tuskers which did not, of itself, solve the problem of marauding herds. Gradually the system changed until, by the mid-1930s, a system of area game rangers had evolved. Each ranger was responsible for a large area and had under him a number of African game scouts. The scouts were usually recruited from the ranks of African poachers and received extensive training in the use of modern firearms. The whole ranger service comprised a corps of elite crack shots. Their task was to locate troublesome elephant herds and either to destroy them or intimidate them so that they returned to the reserves.

This unrestricted 'licence to kill' enabled some ex-hunters to notch up fantastic scores of elephants slain but few of them derived much pleasure from it. It was not the same as locating herds for oneself, singling out the animals with the best ivory, pursuing the quarry, manoeuvring into position for the best shot, and finally bringing off a satisfactory kill. Nor, as a method of controlling elephant movements, was it particularly success-ful. One ranger reported:

'Many elephants were slaughtered, and during that year (1935) one thousand seven hundred and ninety-six were killed in the Southern Province and a large proportion in the Kilwa and Liwale Districts. The scheme was reported com-pletely successful and the Kilwa District was said to be free of elephants, but it was wishful thinking. I believe the state-ment was made to try and justify the slaughter. The following year the amount of crop raiding by elephants in the Kilwa and Liwale Districts was as bad as ever, and during 1936 six hundred and sixty-nine elephants had to be killed in those two districts on crop protection.

'During 1936 a similar elephant drive was started on the north bank of the Rufiji River . . . the idea being to drive the elephants westward from that part of the district to the Selous Game Reserve and to contain them within that Reserve. In 1938 I took over the Eastern Province Range and after a careful survey of the elephant position in the Rufiji District, I reported that although the elephant drive had been skilfully and courageously carried out it was a complete failure.'

It would seem that, until elephants were trained to read the GAME RESERVE notices, they would continue to wander at will in search of food and water. Clearly the solution to the problem of elephant conservation had yet to be found.

Serious reappraisal of this issue had to wait until the 1950s and 1960s. The Second World War intervened and was soon followed by the various crises which led eventually to independence for the African colonies. Hunting, both legal and illegal, continued throughout the period but the 1930s really marked a watershed in the story of African ivory. By then the heroic age was past. The colonial authorities and the independent governments which followed were committed to the principle of conserving Africa's natural heritage. Many erstwhile poachers had turned gamekeeper and, though the problem of poaching has remained acute right down to the present, life has been made progressively harder for illicit hunter and trader over the last two decades.

If one wanted to pinpoint a date as the turning point in the long story of man's contest with the elephant one could scarcely choose a better one than 26th June 1932. On that day Jim Sutherland, one of the last of the legendary hunters, died on the trail in French Equatorial Africa. Since 1899 he had hunted throughout the whole of East and Central Africa. He had bagged some magnificent tusks and pitted his wits and skill against many formidable foes. He was poisoned by a treacherous chief, knocked down by more than one wounded elephant and even tossed through the air by an angry bull. No man had a deeper affection for his African companions or a more complete commitment to the sportsman's life. He only ever lost one of his attendants in a hunting accident and so overcome was he by the event that he refused ever again to hunt in the same area. Sutherland wished for no other kind of life but during brief intervals in his sporting career he won the Iron Cross for helping the Germans to suppress the Maji Maji Rising (1905–7) and was awarded the Belgian Croix de Guerre and the Military Cross for services rendered during World War One. More important to Sutherland than medals were the extensive shooting rights given him by grateful governments. For years he was the undisputed ivory king of East Africa with a virtually unlimited licence, sometimes going on safari with a retinue of 800 or more porters, women and children. Sutherland vowed that he would continue hunting elephant to the end of his days, even if it became unprofitable, and it was his ultimate ambition to die with his rifle in his hand. He came very close to fulfilling this desire: he fell ill while pursuing his last elephant and died a few days later. He was sixty years of age and had spent over half his life on the trail of elephants and adventure.

9

'Most noble monster, huge and black as night,
O Elephant, whose tusks flash snowy white
And guard from all attack your writing trunk.
Alive, your menace puts us in a funk.
Yet, when you kick the bucket, what we thought
Were only bones worth practically nought
Can bring much profit to humanity—
A mace to serve a mayor's vanity,
A table's decorative centrepiece,
Or gaming counters, other things like these,
Or men in colours twain for draughts and chess—
All useful artefacts, or more or less.
Which proves that beasts which, living, terrify,
Become mere toys and knick-knacks when they die.'

Petronius (died c. A.D. 66)

In the Way of Trade

It would be hard to imagine a greater contrast than that between a begrimed and sweating sportsman, waiting, cramped and uncomfortable in steaming undergrowth for the chance of a brain shot at an elephant browsing nearby, and a Mayfair hostess supervising the laying of her elegant dinner table. Yet the connecting link—the commercial and industrial process which transformed tusks into knife handles—is an obvious one. The appetite of the civilised world for ivory knick-knacks is apparently insatiable.

This is demonstrated quite clearly by the growth throughout the twentieth century in the number of elephants slaughtered annually and by the mounting prices realised at the ivory auctions during the same period. In 1925 177,800 lb. of ivory were legally exported from East Africa. This was a fairly average annual figure until after the Great Depression but in 1934 293,800 lb. were exported. Yearly production rose steadily during the next decade. Renewed hunting activity after the

Second World War pushed the export figure up to 684,300 lb. in 1946 and right up to Independence the annual amount of ivory leaving East Africa rarely fell below half a million pounds (these figures include re-exports of ivory from the Rhodesias, the Congo, Mozambique, Angola and adjacent areas). Add to this exports from North and West Central Africa and the incalculable quantity of illicit ivory smuggled out of the continent and the annual figure reaches alarming proportions.

The price of ivory has always been subject to wild fluctuations but any exaggerated changes of value have been flickers on a steadily rising graph. When Livingstone received tusks as presents from African chiefs and Cotton Oswell was a pioneer hunter on the banks of the Zambezi ivory was worth about 23p per pound. By the end of the century the price had more than doubled, to about 50p. It took far less time to double in value again: by the early 1920s legitimate hunters were obtaining £1.25 per pound. The Depression rocked the ivory market and prices fell to their lowest level for over a century: a hunter was lucky if he could get 25p a pound. By 1937 the market had recovered completely and a good tusk had regained its 1925 value. As a result of a sluggish luxury market during the years of world war and austerity prices fell back slightly but the 1960s saw a rapid escalation. By 1970 good ivory stood at £2.25 per pound and later restrictions, which diminished the quantity of legitimate tusks coming onto the market, pushed the price up to over £3.

The twentieth century also saw the whole business of international dealing in ivory placed on a much more controlled footing. In pre-colonial times trade on the east coat was in the hands of Indian merchants (banyans), representatives of firms whose head offices were in Bombay. Many of these banyans had become exceedingly rich by backing Arab ventures to the interior at exorbitant rates of interest. They could, and frequently did, obtain 100% return on their investment in slave and ivory caravans. No wonder a British consul in 1890 reported, 'they have produced a tendency to remain unsatisfied with the modest returns of ordinary commerce'. The banyans and their counterparts at Khartoum, who operated in much the same way, were thoroughly hated by other communities as wealthy and inward-looking as indispensable merchant cliques always are. Their business methods were sharp and their wealth gave them considerable political influence. Yet the risks to which they subjected their capital were considerable: a caravan might fail from any one of a number of unforeseen causes—disease, war, desertion of the porters or the absconding of the leader—and the backer would then lose everything.

The principal market centres for African ivory were Zanzibar and Cairo but when the Mahdist revolt (1182–6) closed the Sudan to traders Zanzibar emerged as the unrivalled centre of supply for the international market. By 1891 it provided 75% of the world's ivory.

All leading European and American importers had agents in Zanzibar while such companies as Hansing and the Hamburg firm of Meyer and Co., the world's largest ivory dealers, had considerable establishments on the island. They provided the banyans with trade goods and were paid off largely in ivory. The big international dealers exported the ivory in whole tusks and in parcels of broken pieces to buyers all over the world. All transactions were made through the firms' head-quarters. Thus Hamburg and London became the main centres of the world ivory trade. Antwerp was also an important market because much Congo ivory was sent directly to Belgium.

There was very little official control over ivory dealing. After the payment of duty suppliers and buyers were free to make their own transactions and export arrangements. While most ivory was despatched from Zanzibar, there was scarcely a small port on the east or west coast of Africa which did not carry on a trade in tusks. The coming of colonial rule changed all that. The mainland opposite the island was divided between Britain and Germany. As the colonial powers developed their territories the principal ports, Mombasa and Dar es Salaam, became more important. Zanzibar's rapid change of status is clearly revealed by the bare details of the arrangements made for administering the British possessions. In 1895, when the British East African Protectorate (roughly conterminous with modern Kenya) came into being it was regarded as a barren, unproductive country which easily could be 'looked after' by the Consul General of Zanzibar and an extra £200 a year was added to that worthy gentleman's salary to help him bear the small additional burden. By 1900, however, when the last few miles of the railway from the coast to Lake Victoria were being laid, the potential value of the new protectorate was beginning to dawn upon the official mind. In that year the administration of the two territories was separated and Mombasa became the capital of British East Africa. Shipping from Europe and India now travelled straight to the mainland ports and Zanzibar swiftly declined into a quaint tourist attraction, an island visited by holidaying colonial officials and their wives who wanted to see what 'unspoiled' Arab towns and villages were really like.

Mombasa and Dar es Salaam had for some years held ivory auctions and now they began to dominate the export scene. In 1901 the Chief Customs Officer at Mombasa deliberately set out to make that port the centre of the East African ivory business. The auction rooms were brought under government control, regular sales were held and were well-advertised in advance, printed catalogues were issued and free passages on coast steamers were laid on to bring prospective buyers from Zanzibar and other coast towns. The campaign was entirely successful; although sales continued to be held in Zanzibar and Dar es Salaam they were entirely subsidiary to those of Mombasa. By the mid-1920s the vast majority of East African and Congolese ivory changed hands on the Mombasa auction floor. After the Second World War auctions came under the control of the Game Department and every tusk legally exported had to carry the Department's stamp. All dealers had to be licensed and only those so licensed were allowed to bid at the auctions.

The scene on auction day at the Mombasa Ivory Rooms when we visited it in 1970 can have changed hardly at all since auctions began a long lifetime before. The unprepossessing warehouse close to the waterfront was thronged with a varied collection of more or less shabbily dressed men, alike only in their wearing of that completely disinterested look affected by all professional dealers. Swahilis in robes and turbans, Indians in long jackets and skullcaps, here and there an occasional European buyer—all wandered with catalogues and pencils from pile to pile of carefully graded tusks and 'pieces'. The ivory, stacked not very tidily on the floor, looked cold and drab and lifeless. There is something very dead looking about elephant tusks *en masse*. They seem to have no right to exist away from the splendid animals that bore them. They lack the beauty of strength which was once theirs when they were flexed against stubborn thorn trees and furrowed into the hard red earth of Africa. They lack the new beauty which the skill of human craftsmen will later impart to them. They are just long curved lumps of white bone to be evaluated by the sharp eyes of dealers with generations of skill behind them, dealers who will, collectively, pay more than £100,000 for those lifeless tusks.

Ivory dealing has a technique and a language all its own. To the expert ivory is not just ivory: it has a grade, a quality, a degree of perfection which must be assessed in determining its value. The different grades of ivory have Hindustani names of ancient origin; names redolent of the creaking dhows and perfumed breezes of the Orient trade. The biggest and best tusks, over 40 lb. in weight, are known as *vilaiti* or, if they are of harder ivory like that of West African elephants, *vilaiti gandai*. Smaller tusks (20–40 lb.) are called *cutchi* and, again, the harder variety is known as *cutchi gandai*. The name *cutchi* is not a term of mild endearment but derives from the Indian district of Kutch where this grade of tusk is most in demand. The diameter of a *cutchi* tusk makes it ideal for fashioning into arm bangles. Since, by long tradition, an Indian woman has to have many bangles at the time of her marriage and since, by equally long tradition, these are smashed at her death, the demand for *cutchi* tusks is unending. *Vilaiti* and *cutchi* tusks come from bull elephants. The larger female tusks (10–20 lb.) are known as *calasia* (sometimes spelled Kalasha). These are especially valuable since the quality and size is just right for making billiard balls. Male tusks between 10 and 20 lb. are known as *fankda*. In the smallest sizes no distinction is made between male and female ivory. Tusks between 6 and 10 lb. are known as *maksub* and those of less than 6 lb. are called *dandia*.

The ivory, carefully graded and catalogued according to these categories, was laid out for inspection by the experts. But they wanted to know more than the weight of the tusks to be auctioned. Each piece must be studied for defects. These may be caused by accidental damage such as the cracks and broken tips which happen when the elephant is digging, or by foreign bodies such as bullets, shot and spear heads resulting from unsuccessful poaching attempts. Sometimes the defects may be caused by disease. This is often shown by a central black spot in the middle of the tusk. A quick smell at the pulp cavity quickly confirms a trader's doubts; diseased tusks have a rotten odour. The potential buyer must examine the pulp cavity carefully because irregularities such as dentine 'pearls' on the inner surface can indicate lines of weakness in the tusk itself which will make it brittle and therefore useless for high quality work.

Nor is the dealer's evaluation complete when he has satisfied himself about the quality of the ivory. He must also be fully conversant with the state of the market. He must know what grades of ivory are currently in demand. Sometimes it will be *calasia* which fetches the highest prices. At the next sale the market may be glutted with small tusks and *vilaiti* may attract the keenest bidding. Then curvature and density must be taken into consideration. A straight tusk is more valuable than one having a deep curve because it is more versatile. *Gandai*, the hard ivory of the forest elephant, is less readily carved than the softer ivory of the bush elephant and is thus not so valuable. Female tusks usually have a greater proportion of solid ivory than male tusks, which may be hollow for over half their length. This makes female ivory particularly useful for making billiard balls, although such balls are now very rarely made of ivory. In fact, dealers are usually only too happy to buy old billiard balls so that they can be resold for carving purposes.

There was a time, not long past, when the prospective buyer also had to be alert to the tricks of the seller. There were various ways of 'improving' the weight of a tusk. Lead might be imbedded deep in the hollow interior or the tusk might be immersed in water to swell the grain slightly. The stringent checks carried out by the Game Department in the post war period rendered unwise any such attempts at deception.

The auction sales themselves are lively affairs. At the one we attended it soon became obvious that demand far exceeded supply. As the Game Department auctioneer moved from lot to lot through the morning and afternoon, the bidding became quite heated, especially for the better grades. Recently there had been a great shortage of ivory on the world market and some of the prices achieved reached new record levels. Even they have been frequently surpassed since. Such is the demand for African ivory throughout Asia that dealers have no difficulty in disposing of their whole stock at very favourable prices and this makes for keen competition. The heartiest bidding was for four magnificent six-foot tusks weighing over 100 lb. apiece but no lot remained unsold and the dealers' interest was maintained right down to the piles of dirty, cracked ivory which had obviously been recovered from long-dead elephants. Even a few Hippo teeth, from which 'bastard' ivory is obtained, sold well.

Talking to the auctioneer after the sale we discovered that that day's collection represented a typical cross section of the ivory coming onto the market. Of the 40,000 lb. of ivory sold about one quarter had been confiscated from poachers who had been caught and imprisoned. About another quarter came from various game departments who have carried out cropping to reduce the number of elephant in their areas. The remainder came from elephants shot by hunters under licence and from elephants which had died a natural death in the bush. It had come from a very wide area; Congo, Tanzania, Uganda, Sudan, Ethiopia—and had arrived in Mombasa by train, lorry and boat.

However, as the auctioneer pointed out, the days when large consignments of foreign ivory flowed into Kenya for re-export were passed. If colonial rule had made Mombasa the international centre of the ivory trade, independence had put an end to the town's pre-eminence. The new African states preferred to make their own export arrangements and some had set up their own auction rooms. For instance, Tanzania now sends almost her whole domestic production to the People's Republic of China through a government agency and it does not enter the free market at all.

For some time after the auction the ivory remained in the government warehouse. The buyers usually paid a 5% deposit on their purchases and called in days or weeks later to settle up and collect their tusks. By then all the ivory would have been resold. Deals made all over the world by telephone, cable and telex would have been confirmed and the Mombasa agents would have made all the necessary shipping arrangements. But the trader's task did not end there. After the tusks had been collected they had to be cleaned and prepared for export and this in itself was a very skilled operation. The dealer had to decide on the best use for each tusk and then have it sawn into appropriate-sized pieces suitable for carving, or making brush backs, buttons, piano keys or other vanities. He had to know his customers' requirements down to the last detail. He also had to calculate how to cut up his precious tusks in such a way that the maximum amount of workable ivory was extracted from each one. None of the valuable ivory was wasted; even the sawdust was carefully collected to be sold to producers of fertiliser or jeweller's polish.

And where was all this ivory bound for? It is still the traditional craft centres which dominate the market. Nearly all the trophies bought in that 1970 sale ended up in China, Hong Kong, Singapore and India. A few parcels went to the Persian Gulf and some were exported direct to Europe. Few attempts have ever been made to establish ivory workshops in the West or even in the producer countries themselves. In 1973 there was only one ivory carver in Kenya—and he was Singhalese. In the whole of Europe there are only two top quality ivory craftsmen. In the East ivory curios are a major export commodity. Hong Kong's chopsticks and tourist knick-knacks are well known and she even exports them back to Africa, whence they find their way to the U.S.A., Germany and Britain in the luggage of tourists who have bought them as 'genuine African ivory artifacts'. In India strict rules govern the import and export of ivory. The bulk of ivory which comes into the country must be re-exported in the form of manufactured articles; only a small proportion is allowed for home consumption. China remains the world's largest exporter of carved ivory goods and her craftsmen are still the most skilful exponents of intricate workmanship. No-one else, for example, has ever mastered the technique of carving those concentric spheres within spheres which appear to be made of delicate lace rather than such a solid substance as ivory. Such age-old skill originated in the well-forgotten past when mammoths still wandered the continent. The workshops of Peking, Canton and Foochow manufactured brush boxes, table screens, armrests, fans, snuff dishes and a host of other fripperies for the nobility and the imperial court. Today the Communist government does not disdain to encourage the production of similar useless luxuries for export to the decadent West. It is something of a surprise to learn that ivory is still in great demand for the manufacture of piano keys.

This is one of the areas in which plastic makes a perfectly good substitute, yet the makers of the finest German and American instruments would not dream of using anything other than genuine ivory. In Japan the ancient craft of netsuke has almost died out. That does not mean that Japanese demand for raw ivory has declined—far from it; Japan is one of the principal world importers. It is only the quality of the work which has changed. As part of Japan's industrial revolution machine tools have been brought into the ivory workshops, which now turn out cheap knick-knacks, copies of old netsukes and deliberate forgeries of fine antique pieces.

The twentieth-century increase in the demand for and the value of African ivory has coincided with the development of various substitutes which it might have been thought would have rendered ivory obsolete. The search for an ivory substitute was, indeed, one of the prime motivations for the development of the plastics industry. As early as 1868 a New Jersey chemist, John Wesley Hyatt, bought the patent of an earlier nitrocellulose derivative called Parkesine. He improved the process in the hope of finding a cheap alternative to ivory for making billiard balls. He produced a number of closely related substances, one of which was, indeed, suitable for making composition billiard balls but this development was destined to be overshadowed by another of Hyatt's inventions: celluloid, the first modern plastic. Around 1900, two German scientists, Spitteler and Krische, were again on the track of an all-purpose, synthetic ivory. By combining formaldehyde with casein, the protein constituent of skimmed milk, they developed a hard, white plastic which they called galalith. It had many of the characteristics of ivory, it could be dyed and it was cheap to produce. It was, therefore, an instant success for the production of large numbers of inexpensive moulded goods—but not as a substitute for ivory. Scientists in all the industrialised nations were now working on the production of new plastics. In the 1920s a new phenolic resin compound was achieved which, it was eventually established, was better than ivory for billiard balls. It was more durable and was not liable to change its shape with age, as was the case with ivory. Since then very few ivory billiard balls have been made (although there are still players who swear by the natural substance).

Interestingly, this is the only example of ivory being replaced by a man-made substance. Many articles—piano keys, knife handles, buttons, mounts on furniture and musical instruments, etc.—are now made from plastic, but ivory is also still used in making the finest examples of these objects. Such is the perversity of human nature that the more a substitute is used the more we long for the original substance. Only in the case of the billiard ball where it can be shown that the synthetic substance is more efficient are we prepared to relinquish our loyalty to ivory. The fact is that ivory has a fascination which is hard to resist. In this it is similar to pearl, the only other precious organic substance. Yet it has many disadvantages: the quality can be very variable so that old ivory may develop cracks and become warped; it changes colour to a dull yellow if it is exposed to too much light. Yet men will endure every hardship to obtain it and pay enormous sums to acquire it. No man-made substance can match it for its smooth, almost oily feel, its soft, glowing patination, the grace and serenity of its carved surface. As long as the sensitive spirit responds to these characteristics so long will hard-headed merchants find the means of acquiring elephant tusks.

10

*'. . . the right flank wheeled suddenly round and swept right across
my front, changing the front of the whole line in a few seconds.
Screaming now started from every elephant, with much stamping
and smashing of timber and rushing about . . . The disturbance
continued for fully five minutes, when the whole herd moved off . . .
On going to see what the trouble was, I found the mutilated remains
of a big rhino, as if it had been first disembowelled and then
steam-rolled many times.'*

—M. Daly, BIG GAME HUNTING AND ADVENTURE 1897–1936

'Truth is never pure, and rarely simple.'

—Oscar Wilde

Stories Short and Tall

Everything about elephant hunting has a larger than life
quality. The quarry himself is the giant of beasts. He carries
huge tusks of enormous value. The men who pursue him are,
necessarily, of above average courage. Their exploits, and
adventures, were they to be written down, would widen the
eyes of the most sophisticated reader.

They were written down. There was scarcely a hunter who
visited Africa for a shorter or greater time who could resist the
temptation to add to the profits of his safaris by writing an
account of his travels to amaze an admiring stay-at-home
public. During the heyday of the white hunter African memoirs
cascaded in a torrent from the presses and an insatiable
readership drank deeply of the flood. A further temptation for
the adventurer-turned-author was the urge to embellish his
text with a series of tales which were more or less true. After
all, no-one would ever be able to check on his veracity. This is
not to say that many strange things did not happen on safari
nor that all hunters were liars and rogues. It *is* to say that of all
the travellers' tales which have fascinated and thrilled readers

for over half a century it is virtually impossible to sift fact from
fiction and equally difficult to sift either from all the intervening
categòries of partial truth. The honest researcher cannot ignore
these great yarns; they are an indispensable part of the whole
mystique of ivory hunting. All he can, in honesty, do is relate
some of the best of them and leave it to his readers to make up
their minds how far they are prepared to go in the willing
suspension of disbelief.

The 'narrow escape' story was a vital part of every respectable volume of memoirs. A classic example is provided by
M. Daly. He was a rather objectionable South African, who
hunted over most of Africa's game country in the early decades
of the century and who managed to fall foul of the authorities,
the natives and other hunters in every territory he visited. In
this story he tells how his presence of mind saved him from a
terrible death in the Lake Rudolf area of northern Kenya. He
found himself, unaccountably, right in the middle of a herd of
sixty cow elephants in open bush country. Some of them had
got wind of him and were advancing with menacing curiosity.
Daly fired his gun in the air in the hope of dispersing the
monstrous regiment of female elephants but, 'they simply
stamp their feet all together once at the shot, like a battalion
of troops jumping to the command and all landing on a boarded
floor together'. Daly was completely encircled and the diameter
of the circle was diminishing rapidly. Fortunately he was a man
of steel nerve. With a calmness which would have done credit to
a *Boys' Own Paper* hero he sized up the situation and hit upon
a solution:

'Habitually, even when not smoking, I carry a few matches
and a striking side of a match box wrapped up in a piece of
waterproof material and tied with string. Managing to untie
the innumerable pieces of string (at least they so appeared to
be that day) and scraping a bunch of dry leaves together, I
struck a bundle of matches, set them to the leaves and got
them alight. The damp air and column of thick smoke which
passed on and between two of the elephants, which moment-
arily raised their trunks to avoid the thick smoke, gave me
my chance and I slipped through. A few seconds later the
rush took place to the fire, which was stamped out, accom-

panied by fearful screaming and stamping from sixty
elephants.'

Good thinking, Caruthers!

It was not far from the scene of this adventure that J. A.
Hunter had a hair-raising experience twenty years later. With
one white companion and his Masai bearer he came across a
large herd in forest country and, singling out a large bull, he
pursued it up a steep hillside:

'Mid way up I knew it would be quite impossible to shoot
accurately on account of the climb, but at length I actually
came within sixty yards of him. Whether he heard me or
not, I do not know, but I have a recollection of seeing that
bull turn and come down that hill—half sliding—but tearing
on, boulders and stones creating a terrible din. There was a
black, jagged rock, four feet high, in front of me and I
rushed for that and fired as quickly as I could as he tore
past on the path I had followed up. I hit him in the chest—
I did not know just where, as my arms were very unsteady.
He never faltered at the shot, but came past me, within a
few yards. I tried to dodge further to the left and I saw his
eyes as he passed, but in his mad rush he could not stop.
Giving him another shot, I called for my other rifle—not a
sign of my Masai, and then I saw another object half a mile
away on the ridge—it was he and my rifle! This elephant
continued for some distance and then crashed, breaking one
of his tusks against the rocks as he fell. To see this huge form
and hear the noise of him coming down the hill were terrifying
and I was lucky that the great herd ahead had not stampeded
. . . My friend had a wonderful view of the whole hunt and
afterwards informed me that the speed of the native and the
elephant, although going in different directions, was similar.'

The cowardice and inefficiency of African bearers appear in
many memoirs and it is hard to escape the conviction that some
hunters found it necessary to persuade themselves and their
readers that the white man was superior to the black even in
the latter's own country. H. Darley's account of a mishap in
northern Uganda is fairly typical. He had gone ahead in pursuit

of a bull elephant and instructed his Kavirondo bearer to follow close behind with his second gun and spare ammunition. After a while Darley gained on the elephant:

'Eventually I got my shot, and he winded me at the same time. Unfortunately, I had only wounded him, so he came straight for me.

'I fired another shot but it did not stop him, and he chased me like a terrier, while I felt like a rabbit. I dropped my cartridges in my excitement, and so was helpless. At last he lost sight and smell of me, and stood meditating what to do next. I ran to where I had left my gun-bearer, and found him on his knees, praying to whatever gods the Kavirondo believe in, raising his hands in the air, and then stroking them down his face and body, bewailing his fate all the time at the top of his voice. The only thing I heard him say as I approached was: "My master is dead. My master is dead. I shall get no more wages", over and over again. He was so interested in his prayers that he did not hear my approach until I was near enough to apply my boot to his person, after which I had to chase him to get hold of some more ammunition.'

The dangers of elephant hunting need no exaggeration; they were real enough and a sportsman, however great his skill and experience, could unexpectedly find himself in the most gruesome situation. Captain Palmer-Kerrison, who in 1925 helped to initiate the elephant control scheme in Uganda, came as near to being killed by a wounded animal as it is possible to come. He was trying to exterminate a small rogue herd which had been damaging African crops. Having just shot two elephants he suddenly saw five more emerge from cover and charge towards him. He fired at the leader but did not halt it. The angry beast gored Palmer-Kerrison right through his side with one tusk and carried him aloft for several yards, before dropping him beside the track. A few paces further on the elephant staggered and fell to the ground, dead. His companions made off. Palmer-Kerrison's camp was too far distant for him to reach it that night and through the hours of darkness he lay in the open, suffering the most intense pain, with only his bearer for company. Before dawn the African had to see off a prowling leopard drawn by the smell of blood and two inquisitive elephants as well as try to keep warm the white man who could do little but moan in his agony. Palmer-Kerrison lived to work and hunt again but it had been a close thing.

This incident underlines the fact that, for all their cursing of the 'stupid natives', white hunters were totally dependent on their goodwill. The wise sportsman made it his business to reach a quiet understanding with his men and to achieve a relationship based on mutual trust and respect. Just how finely balanced that relationship could be is illustrated by another of Darley's experiences. He was passing through northern Kenya when his porters downed packs and declined to go any further. They did not want to enter the territory of the notorious Toposans. Darley reasoned with them and, at length, they agreed to submit the problem for supernatural arbitration; they withdrew to 'cast the bones'. After a while they returned and Darley could see from their faces that the spirits had confirmed his men's fears. But, 'just as their headman stood up to speak, a little green tree snake dropped out of the tree under which I was sitting in my camp chair, right onto my lap. He twisted about there for a moment, while I sat perfectly still, and then wriggled over my thigh to the ground and vanished. There was dead silence at this omen, and the porters, without a word, retired to have a further consultation. They soon returned, saying that they would go anywhere with me now, for the snake had shown them that danger would come near me, but that it would never harm me.'

Another popular theme in elephant hunter's tales was the cunning and intelligence of the adversary. Jim Sutherland reported how he once tracked for hours a rogue male, known by the terrified people whose shambas he trampled as 'Kom-Kom'. For hours the wily monster avoided his pursuers:

'. . . what a dance he led us, through the long jungle grass under the rays of a broiling sun! On all sides the upupu, or itching buffalo bean, twined among the tall grass and every accidental contact with the latter sent the dark green velvety hairs that clothe the bean-pods in showers upon our bare arms, legs, necks, and faces. As there is no method of alleviating the insufferable itching produced by these hairs except by rubbing the affected parts with wood ashes, an impossible procedure at such a critical juncture, we had simply to endure the irritation in silence and trudge stubbornly on, buoyed up with the knowledge that we were after Kom-Kom, the Mighty One. At length, having thoroughly tired us, he entered a dense patch of entangled vegetation and began to double and redouble on his tracks, using every wile to throw us off the spoor that frequent hunting at the hands of native ivory collectors had taught him. When an elephant begins to double and redouble on his tracks, he assuredly means mischief, and feeling that Kom-Kom would prove no exception to this rule, we moved forward with the greatest circumspection. Confident that we were close upon him, we stopped for a few moments and listened with strained ears for any noise that might indicate his whereabouts, but no sound broke the peaceful stillness of the jungle, save the gentle rustle of the breeze among the dense foliage. There now occurred an incident which would have proved a ludicrous anticlimax to the tenseness of the moment, had not the situation been so fraught with danger . . . Simba, in spite of a supreme effort to restrain himself, gave vent to a loud sneeze! [The unfortunate native spoils everything again! Why was it never the white man who sneezed in such a situation?] At once, there was a shrill angry scream and Kom-Kom made a wild, impetuous rush at us from our rear. My trackers sprang nimbly out of the way, and I had barely time to turn, raise my rifle, and fire both barrels into his fast approaching face!'

Sutherland eventually got his elephant. A similar adventure of John Boyes in the Lado Enclave did not end so happily. The 'King of the Kikuyu' and his men had been following three bulls for some hours when, as so often happened in the elephant-hunting game, the pursuer became the pursued. The elephants, having hidden themselves successfully in tall grass, suddenly burst forth and charged from close range. Most of the hunting party fled, only the intrepid white man and his bearer standing firm:

'. . . I put out my hand to the gun-bearer for him to hand me my rifle, but the nearest elephant was already charging down on us, and must have been much nearer than we thought, for he could not have been more than five yards away when we stopped [!] The gun-bearer was just in the act of handing me the rifle when the elephant broke out of the long grass, right on to us, and before I could get a proper hold of the rifle, had snatched it out of my hand with its trunk and smashed it down on the ground, breaking the stock . . . Naturally . . . the gun went off, but fortunately without hitting anyone. I took a header into the long grass and actually touched the elephant's legs as it passed me. Getting entangled in the grass, which was closely entwined with creepers of various sorts, it was some minutes before I could free myself again, and by the time I was on my feet the elephant had disappeared. I shouted to the men, and when they came up everyone was laughing at the way in which we had dropped our things in our hurry to give the elephant a clear road. I had lost my hat, and the boys' loads were scattered all over the place . . . But our laughter was suddenly changed to horror when we came across the body of my unfortunate gun-bearer, which presented a terrible sight. The elephant had evidently knelt on him and thrust one tusk right through his body, which was almost driven into the ground by the fearful weight of the elephant . . . We did no more hunting that day or the next, when the men came back and buried the remains of my unfortunate follower.'

Most elephant hunters were struck by the social responsibility of herd members. It was a common experience to see a wounded animal supported one on each side by two colleagues and hustled out of danger. But the extraordinary intelligence of elephants does not stop there. G. G. Rushby as a game control officer had many opportunities to examine the nature of elephant herds:

'The main tactics they use to defeat the hunter, whom they undoubtedly know will probably be following upon the spoor, demonstrates the elephants extraordinary intelligence. Following the spoor of a herd which keeps a compact formation and is holding to a steady line is, normally, not difficult to do but the hunter must show extra care and skill if he is to get another chance at the wounded elephant. For the herd will travel to an area which has been used a lot by other elephants with well-worn paths running in all directions. From there they go to another well-used area and again on to others . . . it is in one of these well-used places that the wounded one, with a few companions to help him, will leave the herd and go singly down elephant paths which lead away from the line the main herd is taking.

'The spot the wounded one and his helpers go off is skillfully chosen, also the manner in which it is done. At the point of parting the spoor of the main herd will be broad and clear, tending to make the most diligent and skilful hunter overlook any slight trace where two or three elephants have left the main herd.

'One herd of about twenty which succeeded in taking away its badly hit herd bull I followed for three days, and at the end of that time there were not more than seven or eight elephants left. The others had slipped away in ones and twos, no doubt to rejoin the herd bull who by then was probably travelling in the opposite direction.'

Examples of extraordinary luck, both good and bad, abound in the hunters' tales. No-one has ever surpassed F. G. Banks' feat of killing three elephant with one shot (see above p. 129) but Major F. T. Stephens, O.B.E., M.C., Commissioner of Police in Nyasaland, made an unexpected bag while on elephant control. He was following spoor through an area of tall reeds when an elephant suddenly passed close in front of him. He took a quick shot and the animal disappeared. Within seconds it was back, its large head looming up only a few feet away. Again Stephens fired and again the tusker disappeared. Once more it returned almost immediately and received a further bullet. Twice more the manoeuvre was repeated. When his persistent quarry at last failed to reappear Stephens went forward to make sure the animal really was dead. Within a few paces he found himself standing at the top of a steep river bank. In the water below him lay not one but five dead elephants. They had obviously climbed the bank in single file and had, one at a time, placed themselves in the sights of the hunter's rifle.

A number of hunters claim to have brought up some remarkable 'right and lefts'. Two elephants with the discharge
of two barrels was quite common but one sportsman claimed to
have taken a lion and an elephant with a right and left and
another staked his niche in the marksman's hall of fame by
disposing of a lion and a leopard with successive shots. But the
accolade must go to John Taylor. With one shot he killed a
large bull elephant. The same shot startled a leopard lurking
nearby. In its haste to escape the big cat passed the elephant
at the moment that it keeled over onto its side. The leopard was
squashed flat and Taylor accomplished with one bullet the
most remarkable duo of his or of any hunter's career.

Elephant lore abounds in stories of 'the one that got away'.
Many hunters would have us believe that but for a piece of
terrible bad luck or the stupidity of some native they would
have brought down the finest animal of their career with tusks
of over 200 lb. apiece. Very few tusks of that size have ever been
seen but there is clear evidence that such fine specimens do, or
did, exist. Only the bush elephant carries such large ivory.
The heaviest pair of tusks ever obtained from a slain elephant
were taken on the Kenya side of Mount Kilimanjaro in 1897.
They weighed 236 lb. and 225 lb. These incredible tusks were
never cut up but they were for many years separated. Bought
by an American agent in Zanzibar, they were sent for auction
to Landsberger, Humble and Co. of London. One was acquired
by the Sheffield cutlery firm of Jospeh Rogers and Son for their
museum. The other went to the British Museum. In recent
years the tusks were reunited and are now on show in the
Natural History Museum, South Kensington. The longest
verified tusks known to have been taken by a sportsman were
obtained by Major P. H. G. Powell Cotton and measured
11 feet 5½ in. and 11 feet 0 in.

Both these records were established over sixty years ago
when a tusk of over 100 lb. was no great rarity. The chance of
their records being broken is extremely remote. In the 1920s
experienced hunters were already claiming that the big tusker
was an extinct phenomenon. Their modern counterparts now
look back enviously to the year 1927 when out of a sample of
100 elephants shot in Kenya 46 were found to have at least
one tusk weighing over 100 lb. The record for the 1970 season

was a pair of tusks of 136 lb. and 141 lb. shot in the Selous region of Tanzania. Even these were exceptional by modern standards and were shot in an area which had been protected for a long time and had only recently been opened for hunting.

Is it the hunter who is responsible for this decline in tusk size? Has the unbridled greed of the poacher and the trophy hunter killed the goose that laid the golden eggs? Until recently ecologists have laid the blame squarely but perhaps not fairly on the shoulders of the man with the gun. They argued that earlier hunters had wiped out the heavy tusked families leaving the smaller tusked ones to breed. Recent research, however, has to a large extent exonerated the hunter. Many scientists now believe that there is no such thing as a 'large tusk' strain. Elephant tusks grow steadily in length (and therefore in weight) from their first appearance at about two years of age until death. In male bush elephants the increase in length is a steady $4\frac{1}{4}$ in. each year while in females it is $3\frac{1}{4}$ in. At that rate a very old male elephant could achieve a tusk length of over nineteen feet. The fact that this has never happened is explained by erosion and damage caused by wear and tear and it is certainly a fact that malformed tusks which cannot be used as tools, possibly because they have curled over each other, are always much heavier than normal ones. If it is true that the only important factor in determining size of tusk is the age of the elephant then it must follow that the reason why large tusks do not appear on the market is simply that elephants nowadays are shorter lived. Despite the protection of the game parks elephants are dying or being killed long before the termination of what might once have been considered their normal life span. This problem, which reflects more on the framers of conservation policy than on poachers and sportsmen, is one we shall return to in the next chapter.

In the days before every African community had learned how much the outside world valued ivory many hunters augmented their ivory stocks by means of trade. Purist sportsmen frowned on such proceedings but there can have been few safari leaders able to resist the temptation of coming by some cheap tusks, particularly if they were having little luck with the gun. Not that bargaining for ivory did not have its hazards. A. Arkell-Hardwick, who hunted in northern

Kenya at the beginning of the century, records a protracted
set of negotiations with the elders of a Kikuyu village for one
tusk. Having inspected the fine trophy and expressed a desire
to buy it, Arkell-Hardwick was shown into the presence of an
aged Kikuyu and haggling began. Perceiving that things were
not going altogether his way the old man suddenly announced
that the final decision did not rest with him. The hunter was
dismissed and some hours later the meeting was reconvened
under the chairmanship of a yet more ancient Kikuyu. Again
the bargaining went on until the Africans were convinced that
Arkell-Hardwick would not raise his price any further. Then
the salesmen left, astonishing the exasperated hunter by telling
him that they could not conclude the deal without the approval
of the senior man in the village. The next round of negotiations
took place next day and was led by a venerable Kikuyu whose
grizzled head, lined features and generally weak appearance
defied all guesswork as to his age. The bartering went on for
hours until, at last, Arkell-Hardwick rose angrily and told the
Africans that they could keep their tusk. When that point had
been reached a bargain was struck with surprising speed.
Exhausted, the hunter and his men retired for the night. In the
morning Arkell-Hardwick was roused with the news that the
Kikuyu had decamped with the tusk and the trade goods they
had been paid for it. The white man flew into a rage and vowed
he would not be cheated and outwitted. He sent a large party
of armed men after the welshing Kikuyu with instructions to
promise every kind of violent retribution if the ivory was not
brought back to camp immediately. By this means Arkell-
Hardwick at last got his tusk but he was left to reflect that he
would rather have half a dozen narrow escapes on the elephant
trail than submit again to trading for ivory.

In the days when no law prevailed on the safari trails the
dangers and hazards of a hunter's life were so varied and so far
removed from the wildest imaginings of the average British
subscriber to a circulating library that it is little wonder that
the latest book of memoirs was siezed on by a fascinated public.
They could read with a *frisson* of horror how John Boyes after
receiving for many months a daily supply of milk from someone
in a nearby village went to find out why the delivery had
become irregular and discovered that the man's fingers were

dropping off—he was in the last stages of leprosy. They could marvel at the news that one French hunter in Equatorial Africa lived in brick-built house in the middle of the jungle, with his own privately generated electricity supply and his own river steamer. They could thrill to tales of ju-ju and witchcraft. From the safety of their armchairs they could follow the adventurous footsteps of their heroes, vicariously dicing with death and experiencing something of the lure of white gold.

What makes elephant hunters' stories more fascinating than those told by men who pursue lions, whales or other dangerous creatures is the fact that ivory is so valuable. To the chronicle of man versus beast is added all the excitement of the treasure hunt. The hero, armed only with bravery and a good gun may end up on the last page a wealthy man. There is an Arabian Nights quality about the adventures of the ivory hunter. One story that has all the elements of a Sinbad adventure concerns an impecunious Englishman who went off into the Congo alone to seek his fortune as an ivory hunter. He met with no luck and parted with his few possessions in exchange for food. It was in a state of near exhaustion that he staggered at last into a Belgian government station:

'All his clothes were in rags and he must have been a queer sight. The only white officer on the station took pity on him, and after giving him a bath, fitted him out with some of his own uniform clothes, for he had no others to offer. For a week or so he kept him there, feeding him back to strength, and then advised him to get back to British territory, no doubt influenced by a desire to be rid of him, for if anything had happened to the Englishman in his district the Belgian might have been held responsible. Thus the wanderer was sent back towards the Nile with an escort of two *askaris*, who when they got within a day's journey of the river, pointed out its course from a high ridge, and left him to walk alone eastwards to the bank.

'Now it so happened that a successful Indian trader, who had been many months in the Congo collecting ivory, was hiding on the Congo side of the river, awaiting the first opportunity to cross to safety on the British side. He had no papers, and had just successfully dodged a Belgian patrol, and he and his porters were all as jumpy as they could be. Into their midst strolled the wanderer. The effect was dramatic. The porters fled as soon as they saw him, and the Indian, recognising only a Belgian official tunic, went down on his knees and begged for mercy, asking only that the white man should take all his ivory and let him go. Our hero was bemused, all the more so when, his attention being distracted for a moment, the Indian bolted down the bank, flung himself into a native canoe, and made a bee-line for the British side.

'The meaning of the situation at last dawned on the Englishman. He went into the Indian's tent, fed himself amply and turned in for a sleep. Early next morning scores of local natives, believing him to be an official, turned up at his camp waiting for orders, which it did not take him long to give; namely, that they should immediately transport the whole of the ivory across to the British side of the river. The Indian who was waiting on the other bank, on learning that the "Belgian official" was crossing, imagined that he must have committed a tremendously serious crime, and disappeared for good.

'Thus the wanderer came without hindrance across the river, with ivory presented to him which he afterwards sold in Koba for about a thousand pounds.'

And lived happily ever after?

11

'He prayeth best, who loveth best
All things both great and small;
For the dear God who loveth us,
He made and loveth all.'

—S. T. Coleridge, THE RIME OF THE ANCIENT MARINER

'The Kenya Government is strenuously avoiding publicity over the
shooting of several hundred elephants now taking place in Tsavo
National Park . . . Because wildlife is a major source of income,
the government does not want to draw attention to the shooting.'

DAILY TELEGRAPH, 23 August 1966—

Not with a Bang but a Whimper

By 1973 an estimated 12,000 elephants were being killed every
year in Kenya. In May of that year the government took
decisive action; it stopped all elephant hunting licences and it
closed the Mombasa auction rooms to all except government
ivory. The basic motive behind this decision was the desire to
preserve the species and protect it from further decimation by
ivory traders and trophy hunters. The commercial motive was
present also. Tourism had become the country's principal
industry. Large amounts of private and public money had been
spent on game lodges, park roads, transport and catering
facilities. The main attractions for visitors, to whom Kenya
was presented as the next best thing to the Garden of Eden,
was the wildlife. For the first time in decades elephants were
worth more alive than dead. Thus the new protective legislation
was introduced and was copied in other African countries.

It would be pleasant and convenient to be able to regard 1973
as the end of our story, the year in which, to all intents and
purposes, the ivory trade came to an end. In fact, the ivory
trade has not come to an end. All that has happened is that the

shooting of elephants by private hunters has been stopped. Since legalised hunting accounted for a very small percentage of the ivory exported from Africa this has had little impact on the problem as a whole. A considerable amount of ivory still finds its way onto the international market and for this there are many reasons. The basic reason is the continuing demand. In inflationary times raw ivory and ivory artifacts share with precious metals, gems and works of art a value stability which makes them attractive as items of investment. In the early 1970s ivory exports from Kenya showed a marked decline. This was not because fewer elephants were being shot but because Asian dealers and their friends were hoarding the stuff as a hedge against inflation. Another reason for the continued slaughter of elephants is the failure of African governments to co-ordinate and enforce their policies. Tanzania still makes its own commercial arrangements about ivory while over large areas of the Congo there is still little control of hunters. A London dealer we spoke to recently reckoned that Zaire is the easiest country to obtain ivory from because instead of completing a load of tiresome formalities all you have to do is bribe the right officials. Meanwhile poaching continues and government efforts to eradicate it make little, if any, progress. For every elephant killed by a poacher another is shot by the game departments which are still trying to solve the complex problems associated with conservation.

What, then, remains to be said of the men who hunt elephant? The white hunter has almost disappeared. There are no free ranging poachers living as kings of the bush in today's Africa: those heroes of an outmoded folklore have left the continent for good, or gone to farm in those parts of southern Africa where the twentieth century is still being held at bay. Some have joined the game departments. A few ex-hunters have become legends as pioneers of game preservation; officers like Pete Pearson, Captain A. Ritchie and R. J. D. Salmon are still revered as men who, whether they were hunting or conserving, understood and loved the wild animals of Africa.

The development of tourism gave the white hunter a new lease of life in the 1950s and 1960s. With restricted licences there was no livelihood to be made from ivory hunting on their own account. Instead they sold their experience to wealthy foreign clients who came to Africa for a hunting safari. This was simply the continuance of a long standing tradition. At the beginning of the century great hunters like Selous and R. J. Cunninghame had taken wealthy clients such as Baden-Powell, Theodore Roosevelt, Winston Churchill, and members of the British royal family on shooting expeditions. Modern safaris, however, bore little relation to hunting expeditions of the past. Some were the last word in sophistication. The wealthy American or German customer would fly into Nairobi and stay in the air-conditioned comfort of his hotel while he bought his smart safari-gear (tailored K.D. bush-jacket, wide-brimmed hat with a leopard skin band and a gay neckerchief). A small plane would convey him to the hunting area where he would find a fleet of heavy trucks awaiting him. These were necessary to carry everything vital to his comfort—capacious tents, showers, flush toilets, refrigerators, an army of servants, a larderful of food, live chickens, crates of wine—and his white hunter, who was there to guide him to the best game, praise his markmanship, make sure he kept within the game laws, kill off any animals he inadvertently wounded and ensure that he left the country with a fine collection of trophies.

As time went by the white hunters found that more and more clients preferred to do their shooting with a camera. There was still a need for an expert hunter on a photographic safari. Indeed, in many ways the exigencies of this kind of work made greater demands on the man with the gun. Photographing elephants for weeks, with permission to shoot at only two throughout the whole time was very different from going out with an unlimited licence knowing that whenever an elephant became dangerous it could be shot. The hunter had to get his client close enough to the quarry to take the pictures he wanted. He had to read the elephant's mind and anticipate his movements: is the beast becoming angry or is he only curious? Is that tossing of the head and waving of the trunk a gesture of annoyance or the prelude to a charge? Every photographer wanted 'dramatic' pictures and looked to the expert to provoke the animals into making threatening gestures without actually endangering his life. This led to many narrow shaves and to even more arguments between hunter and client.

And what of the elephants? The enormous changes in modern

Africa which have swept away the white hunter and restricted the activities of the black poacher have affected them too—and not for the better. The elephant has been largely delivered from the fear of the hunter's gun or spear but has exchanged it for a more restricted way of life which brings with it new strains and stresses. Game park animals share with twentieth-century urban man one of the scourges of modern civilisation—diseases of the heart. A few years ago Dr Sylvia Sikes, financed by the British Heart Foundation, did considerable research among East African elephants. She compared the hardening of the main arteries around the heart of elephants living in game parks with that of elephants living free lives in the more open highland regions of the country. Dr Sikes found that, when cramped for space, elephants may suffer from the same sort of stresses as man. It had been known for some time that the elephants of Murchison's Falls National Park in Uganda and Tsavo National Park in Kenya were suffering from what scientists call 'acute habitat stress'. Denied a normal way of life the animals developed a variety of nervous disorders which revealed themselves in such physical conditions as hardening of the arteries. It is this and not the activities of hunters which has shortened the average life expectancy of elephants. This in turn explains why large tusks are now such a rarity.

How is it a conservation policy operated with the best interests of elephant at heart has had such unfortunate results? Most of the game parks are not typical elephant country. The bush *Loxodonta* is a wide ranging species which normally migrates over large distances each year, preferring the cooler, well watered montane forest regions. When, almost too late, the National Parks were set up as sanctuaries for them they could only be established in more or less unpopulated regions for political reasons. This has had very important effects on the development and management of all the parks.

Let us take as an example Kenya's Tsavo National Park. There are now about 20,000 elephants in the park, the largest concentration anywhere in the world. When it was founded in 1948 the boundaries of the park were defined so as to include those areas with fewest inhabitants to move out. Generally there were few inhabitants because there was poor land with a very uncertain rainfall. This is quite true of most of the Tsavo area. Such areas are certainly not good elephant country. There have always been some elephant in Tsavo. It is part of the migration route of the elephant from the forests on the slopes of Kilimanjaro to the rich swampy lands near the Galan river to the north before the desert starts. It is interesting to note, however, that early travellers through Tsavo, now the most populous elephant country in the world, did not even mention their presence. Tourists now travelling through Tsavo can be guaranteed sightings of these great beasts. That may be very good for the Treasury and the tour operators but for the ecological balance of the region it is disastrous. Without the most ruthless cropping of the elephant herds Tsavo could become a semi-desert.

It is impossible to over-emphasise the effect on the whole development of the species (and, indeed, of other species) of restricting elephants' movements. The effect of the elephant on its environment is very marked; one would expect it to be in view of the size of the animal. Despite its ancient lineage the elephant is a successful animal and is no 'living fossil'. Dr Fraser Darling, the eminent ecologist, has said:

'Occasionally a species is successful by its ability to be un-specialised and to exploit several aspects of its environment. Man is the supreme example, so successful as to be en-dangering his persistence on the planet. The elephant comes next and again is so successful a species that his only competitor, man, must take special steps in elephant control.'

The whole ecology of the African continent is very closely tied to the behaviour and habits of its two most successful inhabitants, elephants and man. Both play an important part in maintaining the habitat in a form which is suitable for other animals. The savannah, that classic African landscape of open woodland and grasses, is not a climax community as one would expect from the vast areas which it covers. If an area of this land is protected, particularly from fire, then its character changes. The grass retreats, a much more dense tree growth results and this changes the types of animals to be found. Were it not for fire, spread by primitive man to improve the grazing for his cows, the whole character of large areas of Africa would be different. That typical African scene of open savannah supporting enormous herds of gnu, gazelle and zebra was not a static condition unchanging over the centuries, it was a direct result of the interference of man.

The elephants also play an important role in the production of this African scene. For centuries they have wandered over the continent destroying the forests along the edges of water and across their migratory routes. They have formed grassy roads along and between the main waterways and it was to these that man was attracted with his cattle. Once he was established man used fire to further extend the grassland until the present position was reached where the forest is only found in specially favoured areas and on steep slopes.

The elephant has many more minor roles to play in African ecology. An important factor in some of the drier regions is his ability to make waterholes in dried up river beds. It is not unknown for elephants to dig 25 feet deep to find water in an apparently dry channel. They do this using feet and tusks. Once the hole is formed and water has collected in it other game come to drink. In the drier regions the presence of elephants is a decisive factor for the continuance of rhinoceros. They will also increase the abundance and health of all other game in that area.

When present in sufficient numbers elephant also act as ploughmen. Not only do they break down trees allowing grasses to encroach as they have done recently at Tsavo, they also root in the soil with their tusks. This provides a suitable seedbed for a wide variety of plants thus diversifying the foliage available to other game. As is the case with most herbivorous mammals, elephant also act as seed dispersal mechanism. Their digestive processes are not very efficient and a large number of seeds pass out in the elephant's faeces still viable and enclosed, as it were, in their own piece of compost. The Borassus palm, typically found in the dryish hotter regions of East Africa, is believed to be spread only in this way. The tree will only be found where elephant droppings have occurred because they can only germinate after passing through his intestines.

As a result of this sort of activity the ecology of the Tsavo area is being changed. Large parts of the park are being converted from bushland with patches of forest in the valleys into open grass. But having destroyed the woodland the elephants suffer from excessive sunlight and consequent dehydration. Being confined to a small area they have a restricted diet and are frustrated by being unable to migrate. They are bored and they lack exercise. Man, especially the town dweller, suffers from the same sort of stresses and Dr Sikes identified the same sort of health problems.

As happened at Kruger National Park in earlier years, many elephant have entered the park from surrounding areas where they were being hunted. They are intelligent beasts and they seem to sense very quickly which areas are safe for them and they congregate there. The breeding rate of protected elephant is high because of their advanced social structure so that the population has increased very rapidly since the park was first formed. As a result the managers of Tsavo and other parks have two choices. The first is that they can leave the area strictly alone and let the animals and plants sort themselves out. As a result the area will be in a state of constant flux depending upon changes of climate and the movement of animals from neighbouring areas. The park may be a sanctuary from man but it will not be a place where a species which has been reduced in numbers to near extinction can safely be allowed to multiply. In Tsavo, for instance, the original large population of rhinoceros is waning fast and the unusual, though at one time not uncommon, gerenuk is becoming very rare. If the destruction of the habitat continues at its present rate some ecologists think that the elephants themselves will become increasingly scarce.

The second choice the managers have is to control the area by scientific, ecological management so that the park remains permanently in the condition it was started in or is gradually led by clever management to the particular condition where the species which are to be especially protected can be encouraged. In the case of Tasvo, this will mean cropping the elephant so that the population never exceeds the number which the area can stand without becoming permanently changed. As soon as the elephant exceed this number they affect all the other denizens and to maintain the land as it was their number must be controlled.

There are arguments both for and against these two methods

of management. A very lively debate is currently in progress among the proponents of the two opposing systems. Mr David Sheldrick, who has managed Tsavo East where the problems are most acute since its inception in 1947, is a strong supporter of leaving the area to sort itself out.

In general it would seem that to maintain the status quo some form of cropping must be carried out when a destructive animal such as the elephant becomes too numerous; some must be killed to conserve the others. In 1966 it was suggested that about 2,700 elephant should be sampled in Tsavo in order to find out about these problems. No satisfactory choice between the two rival systems of management could be made until a great deal more was known about the elephants and what they were doing. This sample was to be a part of a long term ecological project to enable the park authorities to have the information to affect the ecology of the park if they so wished. But even when the experts were agreed on a course of action they discovered that there was one animal they had failed to take into account. When news leaked out that 2,700 elephants were to be shot inside a game sanctuary there was an international furore. The Kenya Government was embarrassed and permission for the exercise was refused. Dr Laws, the leader of the team involved, and one of the world's foremost experts on mammal biology, especially elephants, resigned. As a result, even today the National Parks administration has no clear idea of how to manage such areas for the best results. Although the lives of these 2,700 elephant were saved in 1966 it is, perhaps, significant that over 4,000 elephant died of lack of food only five years later because the park was so heavily stocked that they had destroyed their forage.

There is thus no simple solution to the problem of elephant conservation. Although it is easy to agree that man should attempt to conserve a species which is dying out, it is far from easy to see how this can be accomplished. The elephant which competes with man must, in this modern world, be kept in its place; there is not room for the two species to inhabit the continent of Africa freely. Yet if confined to restricted areas, the elephants suffer medically, and damage the area they are kept in. The problem is man-made so it is up to man to solve it—and in such a way that the minimum amount of suffering is caused to the elephants and all the other species ecologically involved with them.

Although shooting the surplus elephant population is no long-term solution to the ecological problem, a degree of cropping is obviously essential. It also has the advantage of helping to pay for the running of the game departments. Ivory prices have continued to rise. The banning of private hunting in some countries and the gradual clamp down on poaching makes 'legitimate' ivory, most of which comes from cropping, all the more valuable. Official figures on elephant control and revenue from ivory sales are very difficult to come by, but it is clear that the game departments of some African states are financed very largely from this source.

Thus our story ends on a note of supreme irony. The ivory trade continues and, indeed, flourishes. Most of the money it brings in goes to support those very departments which were set up to preserve the elephant, and harry his persecutor from the land. If there is laughter in paradise this must be an endless source of mirth around the camp fires of the elephant hunters' Valhalla.